Picture Atlas

Cape Town, South Africa

Stonehenge, UK

Venice, Italy

Sydney, Australia

Roger Priddy

priddy books
big ideas for little people

Europe

Asia

North America

Africa

Australasia and Oceania

South America

ICELAND

NORWAY
SWEDEN
FINLAND
DENMARK
ESTONIA
LATVIA
LITHUANIA
IRELAND
UNITED KINGDOM
GERMANY
POLAND
BELARUS
CZECH REP.
SLOVAKIA
UKRAINE
FRANCE
AUSTRIA
ROMANIA
PORTUGAL
SPAIN
ITALY
BULGARIA
GREECE
RUSSIAN FEDERATION

MALTA
CYPRUS
SYRIA
LEBANON
ISRAEL
IRAQ
JORDAN
BAHRAIN
QATAR
SAUDI ARABIA
YEMEN
OMAN
UNITED ARAB EMIRATES
KUWAIT
IRAN
GEORGIA
ARMENIA
AZERBAIJAN
TURKEY

KAZAKHSTAN
UZBEKISTAN
TURKMENISTAN
TAJIKISTAN
KYRGYZSTAN
AFGHANISTAN
PAKISTAN
MONGOLIA
CHINA
NEPAL
BHUTAN
INDIA
BANGLADESH
BURMA
TAIWAN
LAOS
PHILIPPINES
THAILAND
VIETNAM
CAMBODIA
SRI LANKA
MALAYSIA
BRUNEI
SINGAPORE
INDONESIA
MALDIVES

TUNISIA
MOROCCO
ALGERIA
LIBYA
EGYPT
MAURITANIA
SENEGAL
CAPE VERDE
GAMBIA
GUINEA-BISSAU
GUINEA
MALI
NIGER
CHAD
SUDAN
ERITREA
SIERRA LEONE
LIBERIA
CÔTE D'IVOIRE (IVORY COAST)
GHANA
TOGO
BENIN
BURKINA FASO
NIGERIA
CAMEROON
EQUATORIAL GUINEA
SÃO TOMÉ & PRINCIPE
GABON
CONGO
CENTRAL AFRICAN REPUBLIC
DEM. REP. CONGO
ETHIOPIA
DJIBOUTI
UGANDA
KENYA
RWANDA
BURUNDI
SOMALIA
TANZANIA
SEYCHELLES
COMOROS
ANGOLA
ZAMBIA
MALAWI
NAMIBIA
BOTSWANA
ZIMBABWE
MOZAMBIQUE
MADAGASCAR
MAURITIUS
SOUTH AFRICA
SWAZILAND
LESOTHO

INDIAN OCEAN

ANTARCTICA

KEY TO EUROPE
1 NETHERLANDS
2 BELGIUM
3 LUXEMBOURG
4 SWITZERLAND
5 LIECHTENSTEIN
6 MONACO
7 ANDORRA
8 SAN MARINO
9 VATICAN CITY
10 SLOVENIA
11 CROATIA
12 BOSNIA AND HERZEGOVINA
13 SERBIA
14 MONTENEGRO
15 MACEDONIA
16 MOLDOVA
17 ALBANIA
18 HUNGARY
19 RUSSIAN FEDERATION (KALINGRAD)

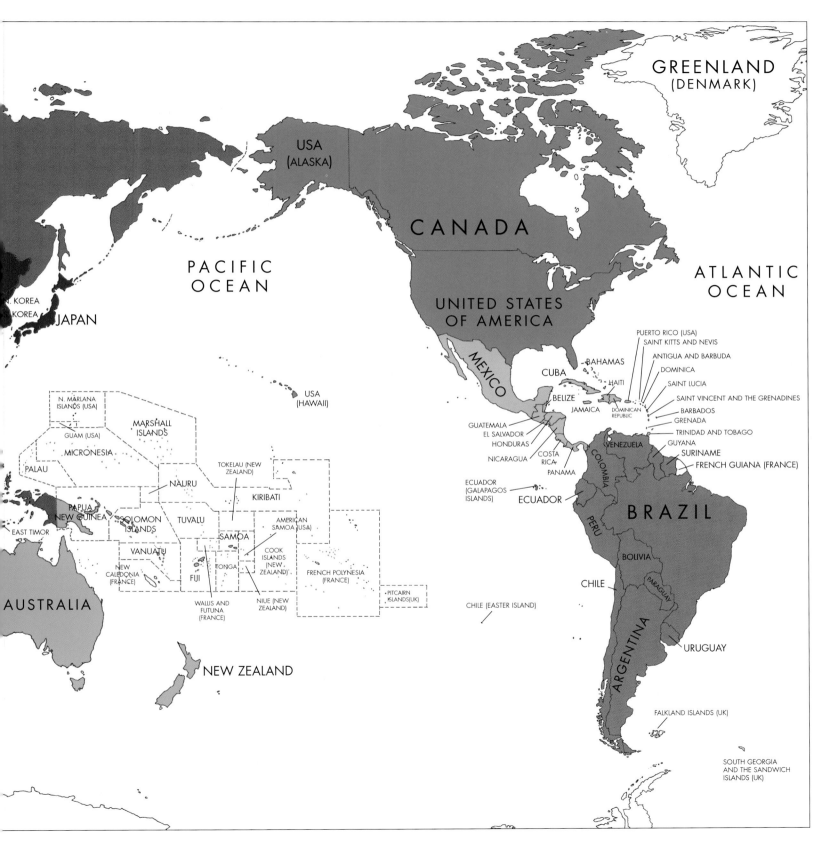

GREENLAND
(DENMARK)

USA
(ALASKA)

CANADA

PACIFIC
OCEAN

ATLANTIC
OCEAN

UNITED STATES
OF AMERICA

N. KOREA
KOREA
JAPAN

MEXICO

CUBA

BAHAMAS

HAITI

PUERTO RICO (USA)
SAINT KITTS AND NEVIS
ANTIGUA AND BARBUDA
DOMINICA
SAINT LUCIA
SAINT VINCENT AND THE GRENADINES
BARBADOS
GRENADA
TRINIDAD AND TOBAGO

BELIZE

JAMAICA

DOMINICAN
REPUBLIC

GUATEMALA
EL SALVADOR
HONDURAS
NICARAGUA

COSTA
RICA

PANAMA

VENEZUELA

COLOMBIA

GUYANA
SURINAME
FRENCH GUIANA (FRANCE)

USA
(HAWAII)

N. MARIANA
ISLANDS (USA)

MARSHALL
ISLANDS

GUAM (USA)

MICRONESIA

PALAU

NAURU

TOKELAU (NEW
ZEALAND)

KIRIBATI

PAPUA
NEW GUINEA

SOLOMON
ISLANDS

TUVALU

EAST TIMOR

SAMOA

AMERICAN
SAMOA (USA)

VANUATU

NEW
CALEDONIA
(FRANCE)

FIJI

TONGA

COOK
ISLANDS
(NEW
ZEALAND)

FRENCH POLYNESIA
(FRANCE)

WALLIS AND
FUTUNA
(FRANCE)

NIUE (NEW
ZEALAND)

PITCAIRN
ISLANDS(UK)

ECUADOR
(GALAPAGOS
ISLANDS)

ECUADOR

PERU

BRAZIL

BOLIVIA

CHILE

PARAGUAY

CHILE (EASTER ISLAND)

AUSTRALIA

NEW ZEALAND

ARGENTINA

URUGUAY

FALKLAND ISLANDS (UK)

SOUTH GEORGIA
AND THE SANDWICH
ISLANDS (UK)

Note to parents

It is important for children to learn about every country in this wonderful, varied world, no matter how big or small and regardless of race, religion or language. For each country, this atlas gives information on population, currency and language, including how to say 'hello' wherever you are. We have also tried to include the main products that each country produces. 'Famous for' boxes for the larger countries provide information about anything from food and drink, to the culture and history of that particular place. The colored band at the top of the page matches the map at the front of the book, so you can always find out where in the world you are.

Illustrations: Brian Delf
Design: Robert Tainsh, Jo Ryan, Holly Russell
Editorial: Hermione Edwards, Simon Mugford

With thanks

I'd like to thank my children Sam and Rose for asking the question "Where is Senegal?" The conversation that followed started the idea for this book. Also for putting up with me continuously asking questions such as, "What's the capital of Egypt?", "Where does chocolate come from?" and "How do you say hello in Thailand?"

Earth Fact File

Continents

Asia – 16,838,365 sq miles
Africa – 11,712,434 sq miles
North America – 9,785,000 sq miles
South America – 6,886,000 sq miles
Antarctica – 5,400,000 sq miles
Europe – 4,053,309 sq miles
Australasia – 3,445,197 sq miles

Largest Oceans

1 Pacific – 63,838,000 sq miles
2 Atlantic – 31,736,000 sq miles
3 Indian – 28,364,000 sq miles

Longest Rivers

1 Nile (Africa) – 4,145 miles
2 Amazon (South America) – 4,000 m
3 Yangtze (Asia) – 3,915 miles

Highest Mountains

1 Mt. Everest (Nepal – China) – 29,02
2 K2 (Pakistan – China) – 28,250 ft
3 Kangchenjunga (Nepal) – 28,169 f

Largest Lake

Caspian Sea (Asia) – 143,205 sq mile

Largest Island

Australia – 2,941,300 sq miles

Highest Waterfall

Angel (Venezuela) – 3,212 ft

Canada

Canada is a very large, but sparsely populated country. Much of the northern part is cold, wild and mountainous or marshy, so most people live in the large cities close to the border with the USA. Huge reserves of natural resources have made the country wealthy, with exports of oil and timber the most significant. Canada has more lakes and waterways than anywhere else in the world. These are important transportation routes (the St. Lawrence Seaway is the longest and deepest inland waterway), and Canadians use them for recreation in summer and winter. Canada was settled by both the English and French, and both languages are spoken.

Famous for...

Niagara Falls
Canada's section of the Niagara Falls is known as the Horseshoe Falls. It is slightly higher than the US section

Maple syrup
The sap of the sugar maple tree is used to make maple syrup

Inuit
The native people of northern Canada fish and hunt seals, whales and caribou

Bears
There are grizzly (brown) bears in the west, black bears in the east and polar bears in the north

Mounties
The Royal Canadian Mounted Police were founded in 1873. Their distinctive red uniforms are known all over the world

Ice hockey
It is Canada's most popular sport and is played and watched by many people. Canada produces some of the world's best players

Polar bears

Totem pole

Whales swim off the Canadian coast

The CN Tower in Toronto stands at 1,815 feet

Map labels

NORTHWEST TERRITORIES
YUKON TERRITORY
Yellowknife
NUNAVUT
ALBERTA
SASKATCHEWAN
Edmonton
BRITISH COLUMBIA
Rocky Mountains
Vancouver
Victoria
Calgary
Lethbridge
Saskatoon
Regina
Winnipeg
MANITOBA
Hudson Bay
Thunder Bay
ONTARIO
NEWFOUNDLAND
LABRADOR
St. Johns
QUEBEC
Quebec
PRINCE EDWARD ISLAND
Halifax
Montreal
NOVA SCOTIA
OTTAWA
Toronto
Hamilton
NEW BRUNSWICK

Maple trees have beautiful colors during the fall. The maple leaf is the national symbol

The vast prairies of western Canada are used to grow huge amounts of cereal crops

Logs are moved around by floating them on lakes and rivers

Population:	33.2 million
Money:	**Canadian dollar**
Language:	**English**
Say hello:	**Hello**
Pronunciation:	**hel-lo**

United States of America

A union of 50 states, the USA is the world's fourth largest country in area. The landscape varies enormously, from huge, flat grasslands and plains to forests, mountains and deserts. The vast amount of natural resources, including fertile land for growing wheat, prairies for grazing animals and minerals like oil, gas and coal, have helped to create the most powerful economy in the world. Every major modern industry exists here, and the country dominates the world's entertainment industry (Hollywood is the movie-making capital of the world). America's rock and pop stars sell millions of records and its TV shows are watched in homes around the globe. All of these things make the USA a very powerful and influential country.

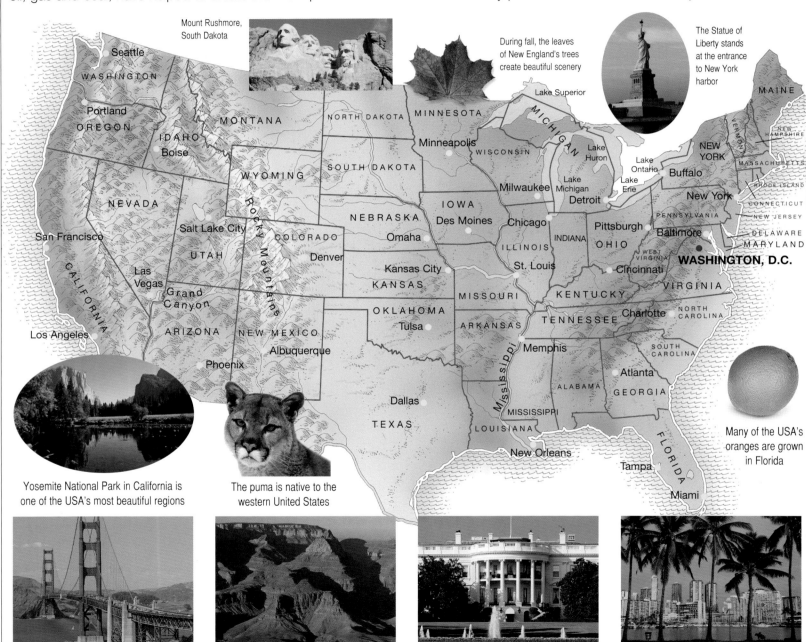

Mount Rushmore, South Dakota

During fall, the leaves of New England's trees create beautiful scenery

The Statue of Liberty stands at the entrance to New York harbor

Yosemite National Park in California is one of the USA's most beautiful regions

The puma is native to the western United States

Many of the USA's oranges are grown in Florida

San Francisco's Golden Gate Bridge is one of the world's most recognizable landmarks

The spectacular Grand Canyon in Arizona is up to one mile deep in places

The White House in Washington, D.C. is the home and office of the US president

Honolulu is the state capital of Hawaii, which lies 1,600 miles out in the Pacific Ocean

The 50 States of America

Alabama	Montana
Alaska	Nebraska
Arizona	Nevada
Arkansas	New Hampshire
California	New Jersey
Colorado	New Mexico
Connecticut	New York
Delaware	North Carolina
Florida	North Dakota
Georgia	Ohio
Hawaii	Oklahoma
Idaho	Oregon
Illinois	Pennsylvania
Indiana	Rhode Island
Iowa	South Carolina
Kansas	South Dakota
Kentucky	Tennessee
Louisiana	Texas
Maine	Utah
Maryland	Vermont
Massachusetts	Virginia
Michigan	Washington
Minnesota	West Virginia
Mississippi	Wisconsin
Missouri	Wyoming

Two states in the USA, Alaska and Hawaii, do not border another US state. Instead, they are separated by another country or the sea.

Alaska

Alaska lies next to the northwest tip of Canada. It was bought from Russia in 1867. Nearly one-third of Alaska lies within the Arctic Circle.

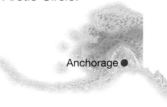

Anchorage ●

Dog sleds are sometimes used to travel across Alaska's frozen areas

Hawaii

● Honolulu

Millions of tourists travel to Hawaii, the group of volcanic islands that form the USA's Pacific Ocean outpost.

Famous for...

The Constitution
The United States has had the same system of government since it was formed in 1787

Hamburgers
One of the USA's most popular foods, American hamburger restaurants can be found all over the world

Disney
One of the world's largest companies, Disney's cartoons and movies have entertained children for more than 80 years

Space exploration
The USA leads the world in space exploration. It made history when it sent three astronauts to the Moon in 1969

Silicon Valley
This area of California near San Francisco is the center of the world's computer industry

American sport
Sport is a very important part of life in the USA. American football, baseball and basketball are all popular, attracting large crowds and TV audiences

Population:	308.8 million
Money:	US dollar
Language:	English
Say hello:	Hello
Pronunciation:	hel-lo

Mexico

This large country has a varied climate, with hot, dry deserts and snow-capped mountains. Most of the steamy, tropical jungles are in the southeast, and these are home to jaguars, boa constrictors and monkeys as well as many birds. Mexico sometimes experiences volcanic eruptions and earthquakes. Music is an important part of Mexican life. Most famous are the Mariachi bands, who wander the streets, singing and playing guitars, trumpets and violins. Many religious festivals are celebrated in Mexico, such as The 'Day of the Dead', where people remember relatives who have died.

A gummy substance called chicle is found in sapodilla trees that grow here. It is used to make chewing gum

Tijuana
Rio Grande
Guaymas • Chihuahua
Pacific Ocean
Baja California
Culiacán • Torreón • Monterrey
La Paz • Durango
Guadalupe
Aguascalientes
Guadalajara • León
MEXICO CITY • Puebla
Acapulco
Celestún
Cancun
Chichen Itza
Yucatan Peninsula

Celestún, on the Yucatan Peninsula, is home to thousands of flamingos in the summer

The Mayan city of Chichen Itza, on the Yucatan Peninsula

The capital, Mexico City, is one of the world's most heavily populated cities

Burritos and fajitas are very popular all over the world

Famous for...

Chilis
Red and green chili peppers make Mexican food hot and spicy

Chihuahuas
The smallest dogs in the world – some are small enough to fit in the palm of an adult's hand

Sombreros
The wide-brimmed hats are made and worn here

Silver
Mexico is one of the world's leading producers of silver

Jumping beans
These seed pods contain insect larvae, which make the beans move

Traveling Mariachi bands provide entertainment at weddings and other events

Population:	107.8 million
Money:	**Mexican peso**
Language:	**Spanish**
Hello:	**Hola**
Pronunciation:	**OH-la**

Guatemala

Guatemala is a mountainous country with dense jungles and fertile valleys. Amazing Mayan ruins and dinosaur fossils can be found here, and earthquakes, volcanic eruptions and landslides are part of life in Guatemala. The country's main exports are coffee, sugar and bananas.

The national bird is the beautiful quetzal. It is very rare, and was sacred to the Mayan people

Puerto Barrios
Coban
GUATEMALA CITY
San José

The spice cardamon is grown here and exported, mainly to Arab countries

Population:	13.7 million
Money:	**Guatemalan quetzal**
Language:	**Spanish**
Hello:	**Hola**
Pronunciation:	**OH-la**

Cuba

HAVANA
Matanzas
Colon
Pinar del Rio
Santa Clara
Isla de la Juventud
Cienfuegos
Ciego de Avila
Camagüey
Holguin
Baracoa
Santiago de Cuba
Guantanamo

Cuba is home to some rare species of hummingbird

Cuba is the largest country in the Caribbean, and its capital, Havana, is the region's largest city. It is famous for its beautiful but crumbling buildings, lively music and colorful culture. One quarter of the country is covered in mountain ranges, but most of the rest of the land is flat and fertile.

Many people in Cuba drive old American cars from the 1950s and 60s

The Cuban capital, Havana, has many Spanish-style colonial buildings

Population:	11.3 million
Money:	Cuban peso
Language:	Spanish
Hello:	Hola
Pronunciation:	OH-la

El Salvador

Volcanic ash has helped to make the soil fertile in this small country. El Salvador grows coffee, sugarcane and cotton and making cloth and clothing is an important industry. It was one of the first countries to use volcanic heat to provide electricity for homes and businesses.

Chaletenango
SAN SALVADOR
La Libertad

Population:	7 million
Money:	Salvadoran colón/US dollar
Language:	Spanish
Hello:	Hola
Pronunciation:	OH-la

Jamaica

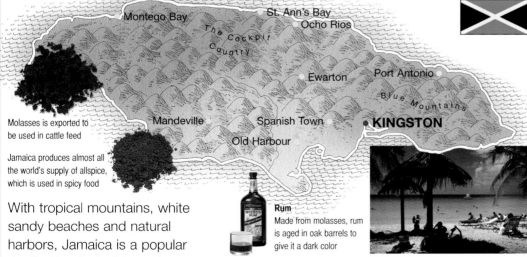

Montego Bay
St. Ann's Bay
Ocho Rios
The Cockpit Country
Ewarton
Port Antonio
Blue Mountains
Mandeville
Spanish Town
KINGSTON
Old Harbour

Molasses is exported to be used in cattle feed

Jamaica produces almost all the world's supply of allspice, which is used in spicy food

Rum
Made from molasses, rum is aged in oak barrels to give it a dark color

With tropical mountains, white sandy beaches and natural harbors, Jamaica is a popular destination for holidaymakers. Sugar production is Jamaica's most important industry, and its Blue Mountain coffee is some of the best in the world.

White sandy beaches and a warm climate have made Jamaica a top holiday destination

Population:	2.7 million
Money:	Jamaican dollar
Language:	English
Hello:	Hello
Pronunciation:	hel-lo

Honduras

Most people in Honduras live in small towns and villages by the coast, or in the central regions where they grow corn to make tortillas. Bananas and coffee are grown and exported around the world.

Puerto Cortés
Florida
Juticalpa
Comayagua
TEGUCIGALPA
Choluteca
Bananas

Mining silver is an important part of the economy

Population:	7.2 million
Money:	Honduran lempira
Language:	Spanish
Hello:	Hola
Pronunciation:	OH-la

Costa Rica

Costa Rica has beaches and swamps, as well as mountains covered in rainforest. It was one of the first countries to attract 'eco-tourists' – visitors who come to see the rainforest, with its many types of trees, flowers and animals.

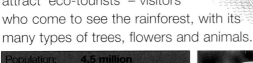

Population:	4.5 million
Money:	Costa Rican colón
Language:	Spanish
Hello:	Hola
Pronunciation:	OH-lah

Coffee plant

Toucan in the rainforest

Trinidad and Tobago

Trinidad and Tobago are hilly islands, with woodlands and valleys. Trinidad has a large mountain range near its northern coast. The country's carnival is the most popular in the Caribbean.

Calypso music, played on steel drums, was invented in Trinidad and Tobago

Population:	1.3 million
Money:	Trinidad & Tobago dollar
Language:	English
Hello:	Hello
Pronunciation:	hel-lo

Panama

Panama hats were originally woven from straw by the canal workers

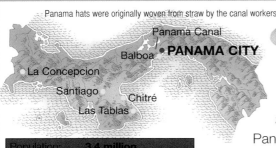

Panama lies at the point where Central America meets South America. The Panama Canal links the Pacific Ocean to the Atlantic, providing ships with a short cut (instead of traveling around South America).

Population:	3.4 million
Money:	Balboa
Language:	Spanish
Hello:	Hola
Pronunciation:	OH-lah

Dominican Republic

This country's white sand beaches, forested mountains and carnivals attract many tourists. Pico Duarte is the highest mountain in the Caribbean. Sugarcane and coffee are the country's biggest exports.

School children in the Dominican Republic

Population:	9.9 million
Money:	Dominican peso
Language:	Spanish
Hello:	Hola
Pronunciation:	OH-lah

Nicaragua

The largest country in Central America, Nicaragua is known as the 'land of lakes and volcanoes'. It has rainforests, mountains and fertile plains. The 100-mile long Lake Nicaragua is the largest freshwater lake in the region. The Mosquito Coast is so overrun with mosquitoes that very few people live there.

Erupting volcano

Population:	5.7 million
Money:	Gold córdoba
Language:	Spanish
Hello:	Hola
Pronunciation:	OH-lah

Haiti

This is a very poor country without any major industry – most people are farmers and barely make enough to survive. Vetiver, a grass used by the perfume industry, is grown here. The country is hilly, with natural harbors.

Perfume

Haiti is one of the largest producers of baseballs

Population:	9.8 million
Money:	Gourde
Language:	French
Hello:	Bonjour
Pronunciation:	bohn-ZHOOR

Belize

Lamanai

BELMOPAN

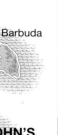

Scuba diving

A tiny country, half of which is covered in jungle and swamps. The jungle is home to lots of animals, including jaguars and toucans.

Famous for...

Scuba diving
It has the second longest barrier reef in the world

Mayan ruins
Those at Lamanai on the New River date back to 1500 BC

Population:	294,000
Money:	Belizean dollar
Language:	English
Hello:	Hello
Pronunciation:	hel-lo

St. Vincent
and the Grenadines

St. Vincent

KINGSTOWN

St. Vincent has an active volcano – La Soufrière. The Grenadines are made up of coral islands.

Population:	121,000
Money:	East Caribbean dollar
Language:	English
Hello:	Hello
Pronunciation:	hel-lo

St. Kitts
and Nevis

Sugarcane production and tourism are the main industries on these tiny, tropical, volcanic islands.

St. Kitts

BASSETERRE

Nevis

Population:	46,000
Money:	East Caribbean dollar
Language:	English
Hello:	Hello
Pronunciation:	hel-lo

Antigua and Barbuda

Antigua has hilly regions rising to 1,542 feet in the south, while Barbuda is a low-lying coral island. Tourists come for the many beautiful beaches.

Barbuda

ST. JOHN'S

Antigua

Famous for...

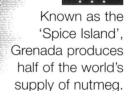

Beaches
365 – "one for every day of the year"

Sailing
In clear waters and natural harbors

Population:	83,000
Money:	East Caribbean dollar
Language:	English
Hello:	Hello
Pronunciation:	hel-lo

Grenada

Nutmeg

Known as the 'Spice Island', Grenada produces half of the world's supply of nutmeg.

ST. GEORGE'S

Population:	106,000
Money:	East Caribbean dollar
Language:	English
Hello:	Hello
Pronunciation:	hel-lo

Dominica

This mountainous island has lush rainforests and waterfalls. It is famous for Boiling Lake – a huge, volcanic, hot water lake.

ROSEAU

Population:	70,400
Money:	East Caribbean dollar
Language:	English
Hello:	Hello
Pronunciation:	hel-lo

Bahamas

Over 1.5 million tourists come here each year

A warm, sub-tropical climate, with 320 days of sunshine a year, has made the Bahamas one of the world's top holiday destinations.

NASSAU

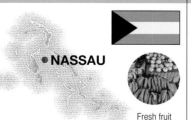

Fresh fruit

Population:	335,000
Money:	Bahamian dollar
Language:	English
Hello:	Hello
Pronunciation:	hel-lo

Barbados

This former British colony attracts many tourists. It is the most easterly of the Caribbean islands.

BRIDGETOWN

Population:	295,000
Money:	Barbadian dollar
Language:	English
Hello:	Hello
Pronunciation:	hel-lo

St. Lucia

Bananas

CASTRIES

This volcanic island has hot springs, and many bananas and coconuts are grown here.

Population:	167,000
Money:	East Caribbean dollar
Language:	English
Hello:	Hello
Pronunciation:	hel-lo

Brazil

The world-famous Brazilian soccer shirt

The blue macaw is one of the many colorful birds native to the rainforest

Brazil is the fifth largest country in the world, and it covers half of South America. The Amazon River flows through the Amazon Basin in the north, and this part of the country is covered by the largest area of rainforest in the world. It contains an incredible variety of plants and animals. Brazil is the world's largest coffee producer, and cocoa beans (used to make chocolate) are also grown here.

The Amazon rainforest is the largest of its kind anywhere in the world

Famous for...

Soccer
Winners of the World Cup five times – more than any other nation

Brazil nuts
These grow in very hard shells

Carnival
This five-day long festival of parades, dancing and music takes place in Rio de Janeiro

The city of Rio de Janeiro is dominated by the 1,296-foot high Sugarloaf Mountain

Population:	194.2 million
Money:	Brazilian real
Language:	Portuguese
Hello:	Bom dia
Pronunciation:	bohn DEE-ah

Uruguay

With low, rolling hills and plains, fertile soil and a warm climate, Uruguay's prairie grassland is ideal for raising sheep and cattle. Wool, beef and leather are Uruguay's major products, and make up 90% of the country's exports. Beef is also an important part of the Uruguayan diet. The rhea, the largest bird in South America, is native to Uruguay.

The Palacio Salvo is a famous building in Montevideo, the Uruguayan capital

Population:	3.4 million
Money:	Uruguayan peso
Language:	Spanish
Hello:	Hola
Pronunciation:	OH-la

Colombia

When the Spanish landed here in 1499, the wealth of the native Musica Indians promoted the myth of El Dorado – a mysterious city of gold. Colombia is a major producer of coffee and coal. The country is named after Christopher Columbus.

Over a million tons of coffee beans are grown in Colombia each year

The Colombian capital, Bogota, is a mix of skyscrapers and shanty towns

Population:	46.7 million
Money:	Colombian peso
Language:	Spanish
Hello:	Hola
Pronunciation:	OH-la

Chile

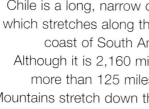

Chile is a long, narrow country which stretches along the west coast of South America.

Although it is 2,160 miles long, it is rarely more than 125 miles wide. The Andes Mountains stretch down the eastern edge of the country. The valleys to the south of the capital, Santiago, are fertile agricultural areas, where most of the nation's food is produced, and most of the people live in or around Santiago. The Atacama Desert in the north of the country is one of the driest places in the world – some parts have had no rain in recorded history.

Over 5 million people live in the capital of Chile, which is named Santiago

Easter Island, more than 2,000 miles off the coast, is part of Chile. Hundreds of mysterious statues are found there

Famous for...

Copper
Chile has the largest reserves of copper in the world

Wine
Produced in the south of the country, wine is a major export

Giant condor
The biggest flying bird in the world is found in the mountain regions

Population:	**16.8 million**
Money:	**Chilean peso**
Language:	**Spanish**
Hello:	**Hola**
Pronunciation:	**OH-la**

There are many active volcanoes in the Andes Mountains

Argentina

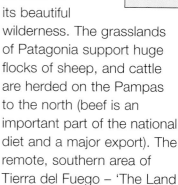

Argentina is famous for its beautiful wilderness. The grasslands of Patagonia support huge flocks of sheep, and cattle are herded on the Pampas to the north (beef is an important part of the national diet and a major export). The remote, southern area of Tierra del Fuego – 'The Land of Fire' – has a large number of active volcanoes.

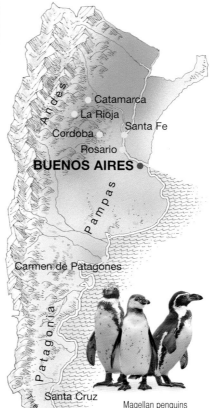

Magellan penguins can be seen in Patagonia

Polo is a popular sport in Argentina. It has been played here since the 19th century

Famous for...

Soccer
World Cup winners in 1978 and 1986

The tango
A type of ballroom dance that tells a story

Argentinean soccer shirt

Gauchos
The name for the 'cowboys' who herd cattle on the Pampas

Population:	**39.9 million**
Money:	**Argentine peso**
Language:	**Spanish**
Hello:	**Hola**
Pronunciation:	**OH-lah**

Buenos Aires is the European-influenced, stylish and elegant capital of Argentina

The longest mountain range in the world, the Andes, separates Argentina from Chile

13

Guyana

Guyana is a small country with a tropical rainforest interior, and grassland to the southeast. 90% of the people live in the fertile coastal areas.

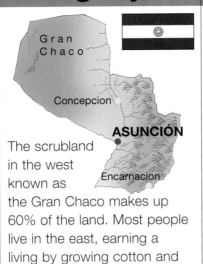

GEORGETOWN
New Amsterdam
Linden
Guyana Highlands

GUYANA 30c

Guyanan stamp

Population:	736,100
Money:	Guyanese dollar
Language:	English
Hello:	Hello
Pronunciation:	hel-lo

Paraguay

Gran Chaco
Concepcion
ASUNCIÓN
Encarnacion

The scrubland in the west known as the Gran Chaco makes up 60% of the land. Most people live in the east, earning a living by growing cotton and sugar, and raising cattle.

Population:	6.2 million
Money:	Guaraní
Language:	Spanish
Hello:	Hola
Pronunciation:	OH-lah

Bolivia

LA PAZ
SUCRE
Santa Cruz

Llama

Bolivia is the most isolated country in South America. At 13,385 feet above sea level, La Paz is the highest capital city in the world.

Population:	9.7 million
Money:	Boliviano
Language:	Spanish
Hello:	Hola
Pronunciation:	OH-lah

Peru

Peru attracts many tourists because of its ancient Inca sites and breathtaking landscapes. Lake Titicaca is the world's highest navigable lake, and the largest in South America.

Trujillo
Machu Picchu
LIMA
Cuzco
Lake Titicaca

Peruvian market

The Peruvian capital, Lima, has many beautiful Spanish colonial buildings

The spectacular, ancient Inca city of Machu Picchu lies high up in the Andes

Population:	28.2 million
Money:	Nuevo sol
Language:	Spanish
Hello:	Hola
Pronunciation:	OH-lah

Suriname

PARAMARIBO
Witagron

Swamps along the coast and dense rainforest inland make the network of rivers and canals an important means of transportation. 50% of the population live in the capital, named Paramaribo. Aluminum, sugarcane and rice are the country's main exports.

Population:	461,000
Money:	Suriname dollar
Language:	Dutch
Hello:	Goedendag
Pronunciation:	goh-dehn-dahkh

Ecuador

Ecuador gets its name because it lies on the Equator. Many tourists visit the beautiful Galapagos Islands to see the unique wildlife, which includes the giant tortoise.

QUITO
Ambato
Cuenca

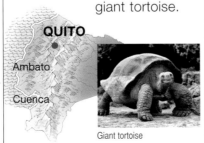

Giant tortoise

Population:	13.5 million
Money:	US dollar
Language:	Spanish
Hello:	Hola
Pronunciation:	OH-lah

Venezuela

Venezuela's economy is based mainly on oil. At 2,421 feet high, Angel Falls is the world's tallest waterfall.

Coro
CARACAS
Orinoco River
Arauca
Angel Falls

Caracas

Population:	28.1 million
Money:	Bolívar
Language:	Spanish
Hello:	Hola
Pronunciation:	OH-lah

Egypt

Egypt's landscape features both dry, sandy desert and green, fertile land along the Nile valley. At 4,145 miles, the Nile is the longest river in the world, and most of Egypt's large and growing population live along its banks which provide water for homes, businesses and farms. The Aswan Dam, built to prevent the annual summer flooding of the Nile, forms the world's largest reservoir – Lake Nasser, on the border with Sudan, is 300 miles long and 10 miles wide. One of the world's most recognizable landmarks, the Pyramids, are found at Giza, which is the center of the country's significant tourism industry. Exports of oil and natural gas are increasing, alongside established exports of fruit, vegetables and cotton.

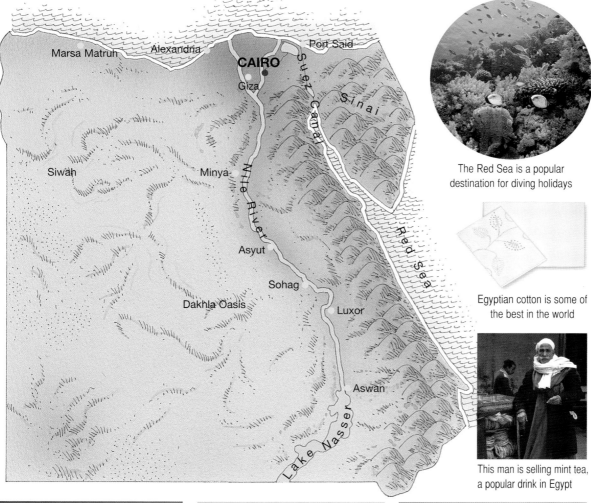

The Red Sea is a popular destination for diving holidays

Egyptian cotton is some of the best in the world

This man is selling mint tea, a popular drink in Egypt

Famous for...

Ancient Eygptians
The civilization that rose to power about 5,000 years ago under the rule of the pharoahs

Tutankhamen
The boy pharoah's tomb, filled with incredible treasures, was discovered in 1922

Valley of the Kings
Many ancient tombs and temples were built near Luxor

Suez Canal
One of the world's most important waterways, over 10,000 ships a year pay to use it

Nile River
The longest river in the world

Mount Sinai
A mountain in the northeast of the country where, according to The Bible, Moses was given the Ten Commandments

A boat on the Nile

Population:	**76.8 million**
Money:	**Egyptian pound**
Language:	**Arabic**
Hello:	**Salaam a'alaykum**
Pronunciation:	sah-LAHM ah ah-LAY-koom

The pyramids at Giza are one of the world's oldest monuments, built about 2500 BC

Cairo is the largest city in Africa, with a population of more than 14.5 million

The Sphinx was probably built to guard the body of the pharoah in the largest pyramid

Morocco

Morocco has snow-capped mountains, stretches of desert and sunny beaches. Fes and Marrakech are ancient Islamic cities with narrow, shady streets and colorful markets. Herds of animals provide hides for making leather goods.

RABAT
Fes
Casablanca
Marrakech

Cous-cous is a traditional Moroccan dish, made from wheat and flavored with spices

Moroccan clothing and textiles are often decorated with beautiful patterns

Parts of southern and eastern Morocco are covered by the Sahara Desert

Population:	31.6 million
Money:	Moroccan dirham
Language:	Arabic
Hello:	Salaam a'alaykum
Pronunciation:	sah-LAHM ah ah-LAY-koom

Sudan

Sudan is the largest country in Africa. The north has a hot, desert climate, while the south is tropical. The Nile flows through the country, providing water to drink and for watering crops. There are many different tribal and ethnic groups in Sudan, though the country is mainly divided between the Arabic north and African south. Sudan is a leading producer of a resin called gum arabic, used in soda and candies.

Nubian Desert
Nile
KHARTOUM
Kassala
Sodiri
Blue Nile
Kosti
White Nile

Sudan provides 60% of world acacia tree seedlings, used to produce gum arabic

Population:	39.4 million
Money:	Sudanese dinar
Language:	Arabic
Hello:	Salaam a'alaykum
Pronunciation:	sah-LAHM ah ah-LAY-koom

Algeria

Most people in Algeria live on the strip of land near the Mediterranean coast. The rest of the country is covered by the Sahara Desert, beneath which there are rich deposits of oil.

Annaba
ALGIERS
Laghouat
Bechar
I-n-Salah
Sahara
Ahaggar Mountains

Desert rock formations near the Ahaggar Mountains in southern Algeria

Camels are herded by the Toureg – nomads who roam the Algerian Sahara

Population:	34.4 million
Money:	Algerian dinar
Language:	Arabic
Hello:	Salaam a'alaykum
Pronunciation:	sah-LAHM ah ah-LAY-koom

Libya

Libya is one of Africa's largest countries, but most of it is desert. The only green places in the desert are oases, where water from underground reaches the surface. Dates, olives, peaches and grapes are grown here.

TRIPOLI
Al Bayda
Surt
Ghadamis
Libyan Desert
Ghat
Sahara
Al Kufra

The insides of Libyan mosques are heavily decorated with mosaics

The ancient Roman city of Leptis Magna, to the east of the capital, Tripoli

Population:	6.3 million
Money:	Libyan dinar
Language:	Arabic
Hello:	Salaam a'alaykum
Pronunciation:	sah-LAHM ah ah-LAY-koom

Chad

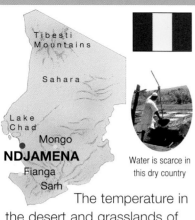

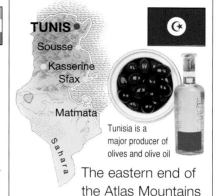

Water is scarce in this dry country

The temperature in the desert and grasslands of northern Chad is extremely high, so most people live in the country's tropical south.

Population:	11.1 million
Money:	CFA franc
Language:	Arabic
Hello:	Salaam a'alaykum
Pronunciation:	sah-LAHM ah ah-LAY-koom

Mauritania

Two-thirds of this country is desert, which grows bigger every year due to cattle overgrazing on the Sahel grasslands in the south.

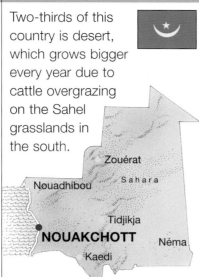

Population:	3.2 million
Money:	Ouguiya
Language:	Arabic
Hello:	Salaam a'alaykum
Pronunciation:	sah-LAHM ah ah-LAY-koom

Niger

Niger is made up of many different tribal peoples. In the north, the Tuaregs roam the Sahara. In the south, where there is more rain, the people are farmers, growing groundnuts, cotton, rice and vegetables.

Population:	14.7 million
Money:	CFA franc
Language:	French
Hello:	Bonjour
Pronunciation:	bohn-ZHOOR

Tunisia

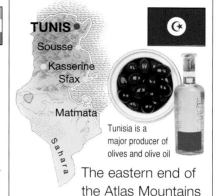

Tunisia is a major producer of olives and olive oil

The eastern end of the Atlas Mountains lies in northern Tunisia, and there are fertile plains near the coast. The Sahara Desert is in the south of the country.

Population:	10.4 million
Money:	Tunisian dinar
Language:	Arabic
Hello:	Salaam a'alaykum
Pronunciation:	sah-LAHM ah ah-LAY-koom

Ethiopia

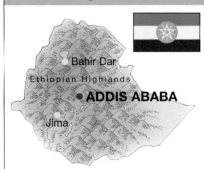

Coffee is grown on plantations in the Ethiopian Highlands, and is Ethiopia's most important source of income. Some of the best long-distance runners in the world come from Ethiopia.

Population:	85.2 million
Money:	Ethiopian birr
Language:	Amharic
Hello:	Tadias
Pronunciation:	tah-dee-yahs

Eritrea

Eritrea means 'red', which comes from its position beside the Red Sea. It is a very poor country – over 80% of the population are subsistence farmers or nomadic herdsmen.

Population:	5 million
Money:	Nakfa
Language:	Tigrinya
Hello:	Selam
Pronunciation:	sah-lah-ahm

Somalia

Old Mogadishu

Somalia is situated on the Horn of Africa, which stretches out into the Indian Ocean, and forms the Gulf of Aden. The country has suffered from many years of war and famine.

Population:	9 million
Money:	Somali shilling
Language:	Arabic
Hello:	Salaam a'alaykum
Pronunciation:	sah-LAHM ah ah-LAY-koom

Djibouti

Djibouti lies in a strategic position that links the Red Sea with the Indian Ocean. The capital, Djibouti, is an important port.

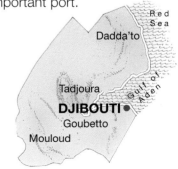

Population:	848,000
Money:	Djiboutian franc
Language:	Arabic
Hello:	Salaam a'alaykum
Pronunciation:	sah-LAHM ah ah-LAY-koom

Mali

Mud building

Niger River

BAMAKO

Mali is a desert country. People rely on the Niger River for fish and water.

Population:	12.7 million
Money:	CFA franc
Language:	French
Hello:	Bonjour
Pronunciation:	bohn-ZHOOR

Senegal

Most people in Senegal are farmers, and the main crop is peanuts.

DAKAR

Peanut butter

Population:	12.7 million
Money:	CFA franc
Language:	French
Hello:	Bonjour
Pronunciation:	bohn-ZHOOR

Gambia

The Gambia River provides the people with fish, water for crops, and a means of transportation.

BANJUL

Population:	1.8 million
Money:	Dalasi
Language:	English
Hello:	Hello
Pronunciation:	hel-lo

Guinea-Bissau

Nuts are the country's most important crop, in particular cashew nuts.

BISSAU

Cashew nuts

Population:	1.7 million
Money:	CFA franc
Language:	Portuguese
Hello:	Bom dia
Pronunciation:	bohn DEE-ah

Guinea

Guinea is extremely hot and wet. Its resources include gold and diamonds.

CONAKRY

Population:	9.6 million
Money:	Guinean franc
Language:	French
Hello:	Bonjour
Pronunciation:	bohn-ZHOOR

Sierra Leone

In tropical Sierra Leone, diamonds are the most important export.

Diamonds

FREETOWN

Population:	6 million
Money:	Leone
Language:	English
Hello:	Hello
Pronunciation:	hel-lo

Liberia

Valuable rubber and mahogany trees grow in the Liberian forests and tropical jungle.

MONROVIA

Population:	3.9 million
Money:	Liberian dollar
Language:	English
Hello:	Hello
Pronunciation:	hel-lo

São Tomé
and Príncipe

The rainforests of these tiny volcanic islands are full of parrots, canaries and kingfishers.

Príncipe

SÃO TOMÉ

São Tomé

Population:	160,000
Money:	Dobra
Language:	Portuguese
Hello:	Bom dia
Pronunciation:	bohn DEE-ah

Burkina Faso

Cotton and small amounts of gold are the main exports from this agricultural country.

OUAGADOUGOU

Population:	15.2 million
Money:	CFA franc
Language:	French
Hello:	Bonjour
Pronunciation:	bohn-ZHOOR

Ghana

Cocoa, which is used to make chocolate, is grown in Ghana.

ACCRA

Cocoa powder

Population:	23.9 million
Money:	Cedi
Language:	English
Hello:	Hello
Pronunciation:	hel-lo

Togo

Togo's main export is phosphate, a mineral used in many things such as cola drinks.

LOMÉ

Population:	6.8 million
Money:	CFA franc
Language:	French
Hello:	Bonjour
Pronunciation:	bohn-ZHOOR

Benin

Benin produces palm oil, which is used in ice cream, soaps and medicines.

PORTO-NOVO

Population:	9.1 million
Money:	CFA franc
Language:	French
Hello:	Bonjour
Pronunciation:	bohn-ZHOOR

Equatorial Guinea

This country is made up of mainland Rio Muni, the fertile island of Bioco and four tiny islands. Cocoa and vegetables, such as sweet potatoes, are grown here. Mahogany and other hardwoods are a major export.

MALABO

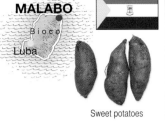

Sweet potatoes

Population:	520,000
Money:	CFA franc
Language:	Spanish
Hello:	Hola
Pronunciation:	OH-lah

Côte d'Ivoire (Ivory Coast)

The former French colony of Côte d'Ivoire is one of the largest countries on the West African coast. The climate is perfect for growing cocoa beans, and 40% of the world's cocoa is produced here, making it the most important cocoa producer in the world.

YAMOUSSOUKRO

San Pedro

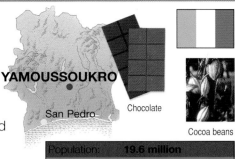

Chocolate

Cocoa beans

Population:	19.6 million
Money:	CFA franc
Language:	French
Hello:	Bonjour
Pronunciation:	bohn-ZHOOR

Cameroon

Lion

Cameroon's tropical rainforest is home to monkeys, birds and snakes, and is a source of lumber. Large wild animals, including lions, elephants and antelope, roam the dry savannah grassland in the south.

Garoua

Douala

YAOUNDÉ

Ambam

Population:	18.9 million
Money:	CFA franc
Language:	English
Hello:	Hello
Pronunciation:	hel-lo

Gabon

LIBREVILLE

Port-Gentil

Much of the interior of this country is covered with rainforest and mountains. The cities of Libreville and Port-Gentil are major seaports, and most of the people live and work in them.

There are many rivers that run through Gabon

Population:	1.4 million
Money:	CFA franc
Language:	French
Hello:	Bonjour
Pronunciation:	bohn-ZHOOR

Central African Republic

The forests of this country are home to rare gorillas. This part of Africa is also inhabited by Pygmies, a race of people that grow to only three to four feet tall.

Ouadda

Bouar

BANGUI

Ubangi

Zinga

Fishing in the Ubangi River

Population:	4.4 million
Money:	CFA franc
Language:	French
Hello:	Bonjour
Pronunciation:	bohn-ZHOOR

Cape Verde

Santo Antão

São Vicente

São Nicolau

Sal

Boa Vista

Bananas

São Tiago

Maio

Fogo

Brava

PRAIA

Cape Verde is made up of a group of volcanic islands off the coast of West Africa. Bananas are grown here for export, but most food has to be imported.

Population:	542,000
Money:	Cape Verde escudo
Language:	Portuguese
Hello:	Bom dia
Pronunciation:	bohn DEE-ah

Democratic Republic
of the Congo

This is one of Africa's largest countries. Most of the land is covered by the forests of the Congo Basin, and the Congo River is the second longest river in Africa (after the Nile). It forms the main transportation route through the country. Copper is mined and processed here, and is used to make brass. This is made into musical instruments.

Congo River

Congo Basin

Ilebo

Kindu

KINSHASA

Kalemie

Lake Tanganyika

Lubumbashi

Market in Kinshasa

Trumpet made of brass

The forests of the Democratic Republic of the Congo are home to rare mountain gorillas

Population:	64.7 million
Money:	Congolese franc
Language:	French
Hello:	Bonjour
Pronunciation:	bohn-ZHOOR

Congo

Congo is hot and humid, and covered in savannah and tropical forest. Most of the population live in and around Brazzaville and Pointe-Noire.

Ouesso

The Congo River

Congo River

BRAZZAVILLE

Pointe-Noire

Population:	3.8 million
Money:	CFA franc
Language:	French
Hello:	Bonjour
Pronunciation:	bohn-ZHOOR

Nigeria

Nigeria has the largest population of any country in Africa, and there are over 250 languages spoken here. It is a mix of a traditional African society, with people following tribal customs, and an oil-based economy with modern, western-style cities (Nigerian oil is low in sulphur and is used in jet engines). Nigeria is always hot, but the northern savannah has very little rainfall, while the southern Niger delta has rain all year round. People in rural areas grow cassava, rice, yams and corn to feed their families.

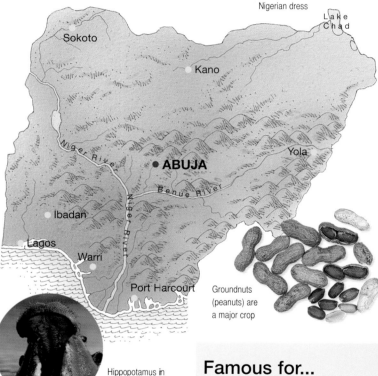

Traditional Nigerian dress

Lake Chad

Sokoto

Kano

Niger River

ABUJA

Yola

Benue River

Ibadan

Niger River

Lagos

Warri

Port Harcourt

Groundnuts (peanuts) are a major crop

Hippopotamus in the Niger River

Women selling spices at a Nigerian food market

Famous for...

Juju music
This has influenced western dance music

Soccer
Nigeria has one of the best teams in Africa

Population:	151.5 million
Money:	Naira
Language:	English
Hello:	Hello
Pronunciation:	hel-lo

Kenya

Kenya lies on the Equator. It has a tropical coastline and is hot and dry inland. Its central plain is divided by the Great Rift Valley. The country has a very productive agricultural economy, with tea and coffee being the most important exports – Kenya is the fourth largest producer of tea in the world. Lots of fruit and vegetables are also grown for export. There are many national parks and game reserves, which protect Kenya's wild animals and attract tourists. The Masai are a nomadic tribe of people who share the land with the wild animals, and herd cattle and goats.

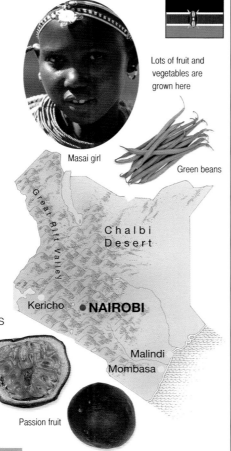

Masai girl

Lots of fruit and vegetables are grown here

Green beans

Chalbi Desert

Great Rift Valley

Kericho ● NAIROBI

Malindi
Mombasa

Passion fruit

Kenya's national parks and game reserves attract thousands of tourists

The fast-running gazelle is one of many animals that lives on the Kenyan plains

Famous for...

Wildlife
The 'big five' (lion, elephant, buffalo, rhinoceros and leopard) can all be seen in Kenya

Long-distance running
Kenya has produced more world record holders and Olympic medallists for long-distance running than any other country

Tea
Kenyan tea is of a very high quality. Most of it is grown in the highlands around Kericho

Population:	38.5 million
Money:	Kenya shilling
Language:	Swahili
Hello:	Jambo
Pronunciation:	JAM-bo

Tanzania

Tanzania is home to Mount Kilimanjaro which, at 19,340 feet, is the highest point in Africa. There are a number of large lakes – Lake Victoria is the world's second largest freshwater lake. Many tourists visit the Serengeti region on safari to see the thousands of big game animals. The island of Zanzibar is the world's largest producer of cloves, a cooking spice.

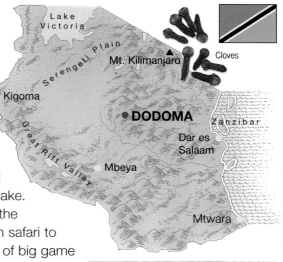

Lake Victoria

Serengeti Plain

Mt. Kilimanjaro ▲   Cloves

Kigoma

● DODOMA   Zanzibar

Great Rift Valley

Dar es Salaam

● Mbeya

Mtwara

Rhinos are among the many animals that can be seen on the Serengeti Plain

The central market on the island of Zanzibar. Fruits, vegetables and spices are all on sale

Population:	41.5 million
Money:	Tanzanian shilling
Language:	Swahili
Hello:	Jambo
Pronunciation:	JAM-bo

Malawi

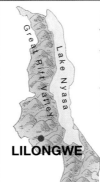

Great Rift Valley

Lake Nyasa

● LILONGWE

Malawi is dominated by the Great Rift Valley – a huge depression in the land that runs through eastern Africa. High plateaus covered in forest or savannah are found on each side of the Valley. The 353-mile long Lake Nyasa forms the border between Tanzania and Mozambique to the east, and contains many species of fish.

Population:	14.3 million
Money:	Malawi kwacha
Language:	English
Hello:	Hello
Pronunciation:	hel-lo

Uganda

Uganda is sandwiched between the Great Rift Valley in the west and the huge Lake Victoria in the east. Most Ugandans are involved in the production of coffee – the country's largest export.

A royal tomb in the Ugandan capital, Kampala

Population:	31.9 million
Money:	Ugandan shilling
Language:	English
Hello:	Hello
Pronunciation:	hel-lo

Swaziland

Swaziland is the smallest country in the southern hemisphere. For traditional festivals, the Swazi people wear colorful costumes and perform warrior dances.

A traditional Swazi warrior dance

Population:	1.1 million
Money:	Lilangeni
Language:	English
Hello:	Hello
Pronunciation:	hel-lo

Rwanda

Rwanda is known as the 'land of a thousand hills.' These are covered with coffee and tea plantations. With 800 people per square mile, it is the most densely populated country in Africa.

Rare mountain gorillas live in the forests

Population:	10 million
Money:	Rwandan franc
Language:	French
Hello:	Bonjour
Pronunciation:	bohn-ZHOOR

Lesotho

Lesotho is one of the few countries in the world that is completely surrounded by another (South Africa). The country is nicknamed 'the roof of Africa' because of its mountainous landscape.

A view of the Maluti Mountain Range

Population:	2 million
Money:	Loti
Language:	English
Hello:	Hello
Pronunciation:	hel-lo

Burundi

Burundi is one of the smallest countries in Africa. Most people are subsistence farmers, where owning cattle is a sign of wealth and status. For a country of this size, there is a large mix of people from different tribes and religions.

Population:	8.9 million
Money:	Burundi franc
Language:	French
Hello:	Bonjour
Pronunciation:	bohn-ZHOOR

Botswana

The Okavango is the largest inland river delta in the world, and is a haven for birds and other wildlife. The country's economy is based on mining, and Botswana is the world's largest diamond producer.

Elephants in Botswana's Chobe National Park

Population:	1.9 million
Money:	Pula
Language:	English
Hello:	Hello
Pronunciation:	hel-lo

Angola

Angola has dry plains along its coast, and grassy, mountainous areas inland. The country has large reserves of natural resources – oil and diamonds are Angola's main exports. Over a third of the Angolan people are from the Ovimbundu tribe, who work as traders, farmers and herdsmen.

Cassava is a basic food in Angola

Population:	17.5 million
Money:	Kwanza
Language:	Portuguese
Hello:	Bom dia
Pronunciation:	bohn DEE-ah

Seychelles

Sandy beaches, exotic plants and animals attract tourists to this group of 115 islands in the Indian Ocean.

VICTORIA

Population:	85,000
Money:	Seychelles rupee
Language:	Seselwa (French Creole)
Hello:	Bonzour
Pronunciation:	bohn-ZHOOR

Zambia

The Zambezi River flows along Zambia's southern border, providing water for homes and farming. Most of the country's income comes from mining copper, although its reserves are running low.

The 330-foot high Victoria Falls are some of the most spectacular waterfalls in the world

Kasama

Ndola

Mongu

LUSAKA

Victoria Falls

This Zambian farmer is harvesting his crops

Population:	12.2 million
Money:	Kwacha
Language:	English
Hello:	Hello
Pronunciation:	hel-lo

Comoros

Comoros is made up of three volcanic islands.

Vanilla and cloves are the main crops.

MORONI

Population:	860,000
Money:	Comoran franc
Language:	Arabic
Hello:	Salaam a'alaykum
Pronunciation:	sah-LAHM ah ah-LAY-koom

Mozambique

Pemba

Cabora Bassa Dam

Quelimane

MAPUTO

There are more than 60 rivers flowing through Mozambique, including the Zambezi and Limpopo – two of the longest in Africa. The Cabora Bassa Dam on the Zambezi River is used to control the water supply to the biggest hydroelectric power plant on the continent. Most of the electricity that it produces is sold to neighboring countries, including South Africa and Zimbabwe. Most people living in Mozambique grow crops to feed their families.

Shrimp is Mozambique's largest export

Population:	21.8 million
Money:	Metical
Language:	Portuguese
Hello:	Bom dia
Pronunciation:	bohn DEE-ah

Mauritius

PORT LOUIS This mountainous, volcanic island is surrounded by coral reefs. Half of the land is planted with sugarcane.

Population:	1.3 million
Money:	Mauritian rupee
Language:	English
Hello:	Hello
Pronunciation:	hel-lo

Madagascar

Madagascar is the fourth largest island in the world. Its tropical rainforests attract scientists to study species of animals and plants that are found nowhere else on earth. Half of the world's supply of vanilla comes from Madagascar. The bean pods from the vanilla orchid are dried and used to flavor ice cream, chocolate and cakes.

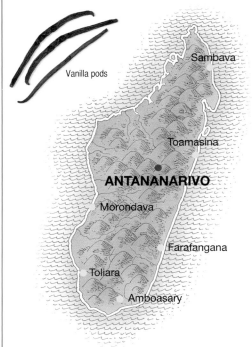

Vanilla pods

Sambava
Toamasina
ANTANANARIVO
Morondava
Farafangana
Toliara
Amboasary

Many different species of chameleon are found on Madagascar

Population:	20.2 million
Money:	**Ariary**
Language:	**French**
Hello:	**Bonjour**
Pronunciation:	**bohn-ZHOOR**

Namibia

Thick fogs are common along the coast, but most of Namibia is extremely hot and dry (the country has two deserts – the Namib and the Kalahari). Namibia has rich reserves of minerals, and diamonds are the country's most important export.

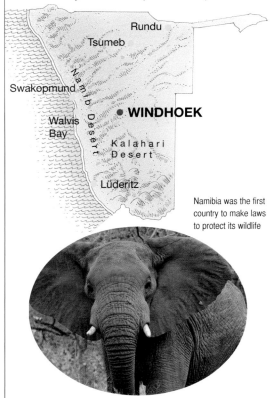

Rundu
Tsumeb
Swakopmund
Namib Desert
Walvis Bay
WINDHOEK
Kalahari Desert
Lüderitz

Namibia was the first country to make laws to protect its wildlife

Metals in the ground give the Namib desert its red coloring

Population:	2.1 million
Money:	**Nambian dollar**
Language:	**English**
Hello:	**Hello**
Pronunciation:	**hel-lo**

Zimbabwe

Zimbabwe's national parks and game reserves are home to some of the world's most endangered animals, including the king cheetah, and both black and white rhinos. Victoria Falls, on the Zambezi River, attracts many foreign tourists.

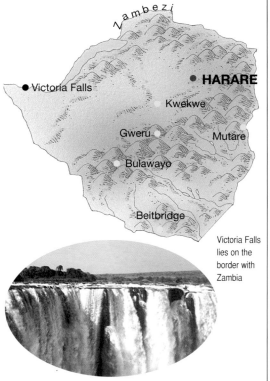

Zambezi
Victoria Falls
HARARE
Kwekwe
Gweru
Mutare
Bulawayo
Beitbridge

Victoria Falls lies on the border with Zambia

The king cheetah is the world's rarest big cat

Population:	13.5 million
Money:	**Zimbabwe dollar**
Language:	**English**
Hello:	**Hello**
Pronunciation:	**hel-lo**

South Africa

South Africa has a very varied and dramatic landscape. Spectacular mountain ranges (such as the Great Karoo in the south and the Drakensberg in the east) separate the coast from dry, semi-desert plains and fertile land. The temperate climate, with warm summers and cool winters, is perfect for growing fruit and vegetables, and this accounts for a large part of the country's economy. It has huge resources of minerals, and mining has helped it become the wealthiest country in Africa. Tourists come to see the beautiful scenery and incredible wildlife. There are 11 official languages spoken in South Africa, and people are still adjusting to life after apartheid – a system that divided the country between black and white people.

Famous for...

Diamonds
South Africa leads the world diamond market

Safari
Lions, leopards, elephants, rhinos and buffalo (the 'big five') can all be seen in South Africa

Fruit
Citrus fruits, grapes and apples are just some of the fruits that are grown here and exported

Beaches
Sunbathers and surfers consider them some of the best in the world

Sport
Soccer, rugby and cricket are the three most popular sports in South Africa

Whale watching
Many species of whale, dolphin and shark swim close to South Africa's shores

Wine
The vineyards around Cape Town have been producing wines for centuries. Some of the best wines in the world are made here

Population:	**48.8 million**
Money:	**Rand**
Language:	**Zulu**
Hello:	**Sawubona**
Pronunciation:	**sa-wu-bon-a**

Ostriches live in the grasslands

South Africa is the world's largest gold producer

Polokwane

● **PRETORIA**

Johannesburg

Kimberley

Harrismith

Orange River

BLOEMFONTEIN

Lesotho

Pietermaritzburg

Durban

Middelburg

Drakensberg Mountains

Great Karoo

Port Elizabeth

● **CAPE TOWN**   George

Cape of Good Hope

Tourists can take a cable car to the top of Table Mountain, in Cape Town

Zebras drinking at a waterhole in one of South Africa's many game parks

Cheetahs – the fastest cats in the world – are found in South Africa

United Kingdom

The United Kingdom is made up of four nations – England, Wales, Scotland and Northern Ireland. Separated from continental Europe by the English Channel, it has a mild climate with plenty of rain, and the landscape is mostly lush and green. It is a major financial center – London is home to one of the world's largest stock exchanges, and also a world leader in science, technology and medicine. The United Kingdom is one of the most densely populated countries in the world, and its towns and cities are home to a mix of races from every continent.

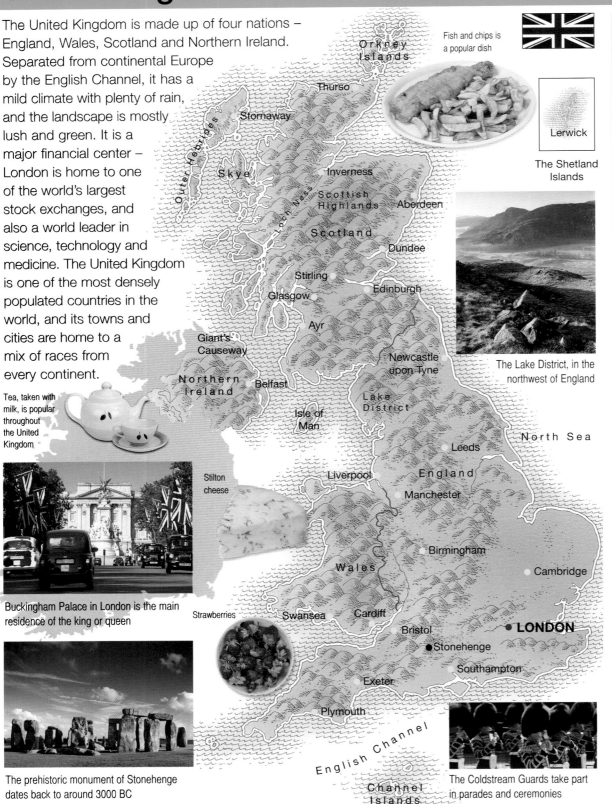

Fish and chips is a popular dish

Lerwick

The Shetland Islands

Orkney Islands
Thurso
Stornaway
Outer Hebrides
Skye
Inverness
Scottish Highlands
Aberdeen
Scotland
Dundee
Stirling
Glasgow
Edinburgh
Ayr
Giant's Causeway
Newcastle upon Tyne
Northern Ireland
Belfast
Lake District
Isle of Man
North Sea
Leeds
Liverpool
England
Manchester
Birmingham
Wales
Cambridge
Swansea
Cardiff
Bristol
• LONDON
• Stonehenge
Southampton
Exeter
Plymouth
English Channel
Channel Islands
Loch Ness

The Lake District, in the northwest of England

Tea, taken with milk, is popular throughout the United Kingdom

Buckingham Palace in London is the main residence of the king or queen

Stilton cheese

Strawberries

The prehistoric monument of Stonehenge dates back to around 3000 BC

The Coldstream Guards take part in parades and ceremonies

Famous for...

England

Sports
Soccer, cricket and rugby were all invented here

Shakespeare
The most famous English-language poet and playwright was born here

Museums
England is home to many great museums and London's British Museum is one of the world's biggest and finest

Northern Ireland

Giant's Causeway
Unusual volcanic rock formations on the northern coast

Scotland

Golf
Home to the world's oldest golf courses

Wales

Singing
Wales has produced many great singers

Rugby
It is the national sport of Wales

Population:	61 million
Money:	Pound sterling
Language:	English
Hello:	Hello
Pronunciation:	hel-lo

Ireland

Ireland is known as the 'Emerald Isle', because heavy rain throughout the year makes the landscape a brilliant green color. The plains in the middle of the country are very fertile and are used for growing wheat, barley and potatoes. The lush grass is perfect for raising animals – in particular cattle for their meat and dairy products. Ireland's inland rivers and lakes are famous for their salmon and trout fishing, and in the winter ducks and geese migrate to Ireland from Greenland and Canada. The arts are very important to the Irish, who are well-known for their writers and thriving film industry. Music, often played on a fiddle or a tin whistle, is a lively part of Irish culture.

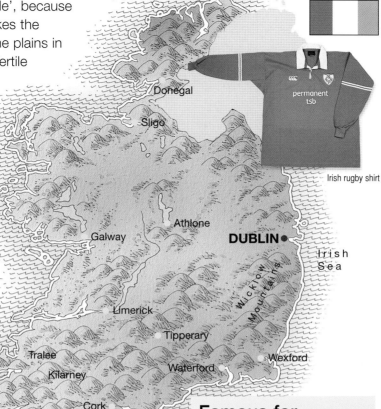

Donegal
Sligo
Athlone
Galway
DUBLIN
Irish Sea
Wicklow Mountains
Limerick
Tipperary
Tralee
Waterford
Wexford
Kilarney
Cork
Bantry

Irish rugby shirt

Johnstown Castle in Wexford, on the southeast coast of Ireland

The Irish are passionate about horse racing and many racehorse breeders are based here

Ha'penny Bridge, which crosses the Liffey River in Dublin's city center

The Celtic cross is a familiar sight at religious sites across Ireland

Famous for...

Stout
Dark, almost-black beer made from roasted malt barley. The most famous stout is Guinness

St. Patrick's Day
Irish people all over the world celebrate their country's patron saint each year on March 17

Potatoes
Potatoes grow well in the wet climate of Ireland. They are the country's most important agricultural product

Population:	4.4 million
Money:	**Euro**
Language:	**English**
Hello:	**Hello**
Pronunciation:	**hel-lo**

Iceland

Iceland is the most western island in Europe. There are huge glaciers, hot springs, geysers and active volcanoes. Geothermal energy is used to provide free heating for Icelanders. Fishing is the most important industry.

Ísafjördur
Húsavík
REYKJAVIK
Vatnajökull
Keflavík

The many active volcanoes cause spectacular geysers

Vatnajökull, in the southern half of the country, is the biggest glacier in Europe

Population:	304,000
Money:	**Icelandic krona**
Language:	**Icelandic**
Hello:	**Hallo**
Pronunciation:	**hal-lo**

Denmark

Denmark is a flat country, made up of the Jutland Peninsula and more than 400 other islands. The climate is mild, with wet and windy winters and cool summers. Agriculture, particularly pig-farming, is an important part of the economy. Danish pork products – bacon, sausages and salami – are famous all over the world. Denmark also has a well-developed, high-tech economy.

The Danish capital, Copenhagen, has many brightly-colored old buildings

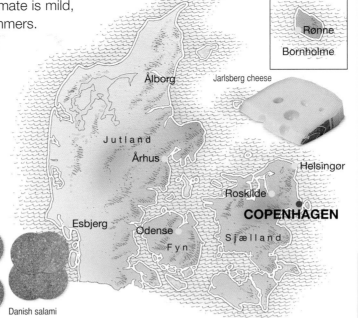

Rønne
Bornholme
Ålborg
Jarlsberg cheese
Jutland
Århus
Helsingør
Roskilde
COPENHAGEN
Esbjerg
Odense
Fyn
Sjælland

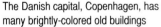

Danish salami

Famous for...

Lego
The toy was invented by Danish carpenter Ole Kirk Christiansen

Pastries
Millions of people enjoy sweet, buttery Danish pastries with their morning coffee

Hans Christian Andersen
The writer was born in Odense in 1805. There is a statue of one of his characters, the Little Mermaid, in Copenhagen

Population:	**5.5 million**
Money:	**Danish krone**
Language:	**Danish**
Hello:	**God dag**
Pronunciation:	**goh-da**

Norway

Norway has a long, rugged coastline with many islands and steep-sided inlets called fjords. The northern area inside the Arctic Circle has practically continuous daylight from May to July, but is dark almost all day during midwinter. Some of the largest glaciers in Europe are found in the mountains and there are many striking rivers, lakes and waterfalls. Oil, gas and fishing form the basis of the economy. Reindeer, wolves and polar bears can all be found in the north.

Oslo is Norway's biggest city and the oldest capital in Scandinavia

Hammerfest
Lapland
Narvik
Å

The northern and eastern parts of Norway experience very cold winters

Trondheim
Bergen
OSLO
Stavanger
Kristiansand

Norway has become Europe's largest exporter of oil and gas

Famous for...

Skiing
Nordic (cross-country) skiing and ski-jumping were both invented here

Å
This small town has the world's shortest place name

Laplanders
The native people of Lapland, part of which is in northern Norway. Also known as the Sami people, most live a traditional life, herding reindeer in the far north

Population:	**4.7 million**
Money:	**Norwegian krone**
Language:	**Norwegian**
Hello:	**God dag**
Pronunciation:	**goo-dagh**

Sweden

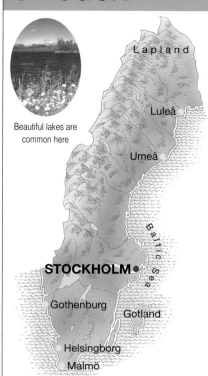

Beautiful lakes are common here

In the winter months, Sweden's rolling hills are covered in snow and its many lakes and rivers ice over (skiing and skating are popular winter pastimes). There is a strong, industrial based economy, with companies producing many high-tech products. Sweden's economic success has made it a wealthy country, and its people enjoy one of the highest standards of living in the world. Large forests produce wood, used for making furniture and paper. The many rivers provide the country with a means of producing hydroelectric power.

Traditional houses have steeply sloping roofs so that snow will slide off in winter

The Swedish capital, Stockholm, is an important seaport

Famous for...

Alfred Nobel
He set up the foundation that awards prizes for peace, science and literature

Pippi Longstocking
The popular books, written by Astrid Lindgren, have been translated into 60 languages

Furniture
Known for its well designed and low-cost products, IKEA is a very successful company

Population:	9.2 million
Money:	Swedish krona
Language:	Swedish
Hello:	God dag
Pronunciation:	goo dahg

Finland

Finland has over 60,000 lakes and many hills covered in forests. Timber forms the basis of the Finnish economy – papermaking and furniture production are the major industries here. The timber is transported using a canal system that links the many lakes. Finland also has a highly-developed telecommunications industry, and many of the latest cell phones are designed and produced here. In the spring and fall, Finland is one of the best places to see the northern lights – a spectacular natural light show.

The northern lights are caused by solar winds colliding with the Earth's magnetic field

Helsinki is built on a peninsula, so many buildings face the waterfront

Finland is a world leader in cell phone technology

Famous for...

Saunas
The steam bath was invented in Finland around 1,000 years ago

Lakes and rivers
Known as the 'land of a thousand lakes', water covers about 10% of the country

Paper production
Finland produces most of the paper used in newspapers across Europe

Population:	5.3 million
Money:	Euro
Language:	Finnish
Hello:	Terve
Pronunciation:	TER-vey

Estonia

Estonia is a flat, boggy country with pine and spruce forests which are home to many rare animals, including the European flying squirrel. Lake Peipus, on the border with Russia, is one of the largest lakes in Europe.

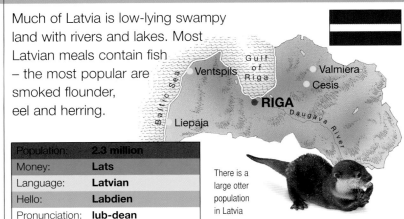

TALLINN
Kohtla-Järve
Hiiumaa Haapsalu
Lake Peipus
Saaremaa Pämu Viljandi

Population:	1.3 million
Money:	Kroon
Language:	Estonian
Hello:	Tere
Pronunciation:	TER-vey

Blood sausages made from pigs are an Estonian speciality

Latvia

Much of Latvia is low-lying swampy land with rivers and lakes. Most Latvian meals contain fish – the most popular are smoked flounder, eel and herring.

Gulf of Riga
Ventspils Valmiera
Cesis
Baltic Sea
RIGA
Liepaja Daugava River

Population:	2.3 million
Money:	Lats
Language:	Latvian
Hello:	Labdien
Pronunciation:	lub-dean

There is a large otter population in Latvia

Lithuania

Most of the world's amber (the fossilized sap of ancient trees), is supplied by Lithuania. Sheets of amber lie on the bed of the Baltic Sea, and stormy weather washes it onto the country's 'Amber Coast'.

Amber Coast
Siauliai
Panevezys
Kaunas
VILNIUS

Population:	3.4 million
Money:	Litas
Language:	Lithuanian
Hello:	Labas
Pronunciation:	lah-bahs

Amber

Luxembourg

Luxembourg is a tiny industrialized country with the highest standard of living in Europe. There are many castles and medieval villages, and the Ardennes Mountains are a popular destination for skiers.

Ardennes
Echternach
LUXEMBOURG
Moselle Valley

A square in the town of Echternach

Population:	472,000
Money:	Euro
Language:	French
Hello:	Bonjour
Pronunciation:	bohn-ZHOOR

Liechtenstein

This tiny country is only 20 miles long and 5 miles wide. It lies between the Rhine valley and the foothills of the Tirolean Alps. Much of the country is forested. International banks attract foreign workers, mainly from Germany and Switzerland. Skiing is a popular tourist activity in winter.

VADUZ
Triesenberg
Balzers

Vaduz Castle in the capital

Population:	35,000
Money:	Swiss franc
Language:	German
Hello:	Guten Tag
Pronunciation:	GOOT-en tahk

Monaco

Monaco has been ruled by the Grimaldi family for about 700 years. It is a major business center and attracts many very rich visitors.

Monte Carlo

Monaco is famous for its casinos, yacht harbor and Grand Prix racing circuit

Population:	32,000
Money:	Euro
Language:	French
Hello:	Bonjour
Pronunciation:	bohn-ZHOOR

Netherlands

The Netherlands are also known as Holland, but strictly speaking this is just the area around Amsterdam. It is a very flat land, much of which is below sea level. For centuries, barriers called dykes have been used to keep out the sea and reclaim some of the land. Agriculture and food processing makes up a large part of the Dutch economy. Rotterdam is Europe's biggest seaport, with over 30,000 ships using the port each year. Its position allows ships easy access to the Rhine River, which is an important trade route into northern Europe.

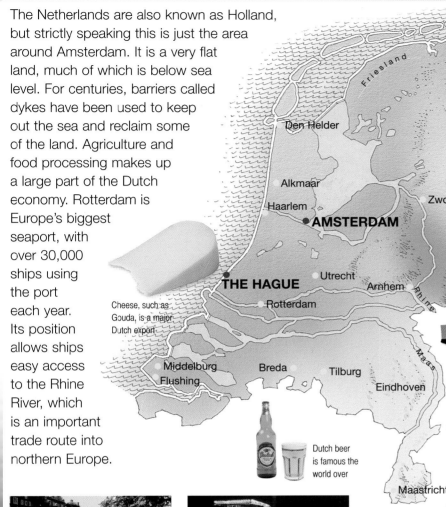

Friesland

Groningen

Den Helder

Alkmaar

Haarlem

Zwolle

AMSTERDAM

Enschede

Utrecht

THE HAGUE

Arnhem

Rhine

Cheese, such as Gouda, is a major Dutch export

Rotterdam

Maas

Middelburg

Breda

Tilburg

Flushing

Eindhoven

Maastricht

Soccer is popular, and the national team is well-supported

Dutch beer is famous the world over

Diamonds are brought to Amsterdam to be cut and polished. The city specializes in the diamond trade

The flat countryside and many cycle routes have made traveling by bike very popular

Amsterdam is built on many islands and is one of the world's great canal cities

Famous for...

Artists
Dutch painters Rembrandt and Vincent Van Gogh are two of the best known artists in history

Two capitals
Amsterdam is the capital city, but the government is based in The Hague

Skating
Ice skating is a popular pastime

Royal family
The Royal family is well-loved throughout the Netherlands

Tulips
The brightly-colored flowers are exported all over the world

Windmills
Many windmills can be seen in the flat Dutch landscape

Population:	16.5 million
Money:	**Euro**
Language:	**Dutch**
Hello:	**Goedendag**
Pronunciation:	**goh-dehn-dahkh**

Belgium

Belgium has flat, fertile plains in the north and rugged mountains in the south. The country is divided between two peoples – the Flemings in the north, who speak Flemish, and the French-speaking Walloons in the south.

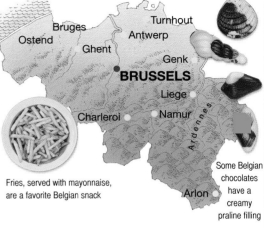

Bruges

Turnhout

Ostend

Antwerp

Ghent

Genk

BRUSSELS

Liege

Charleroi

Namur

Ardennes

Arlon

Fries, served with mayonnaise, are a favorite Belgian snack

Some Belgian chocolates have a creamy praline filling

The headquarters of the European Union (EU) is based in Brussels

Bruges is one of the best preserved medieval cities in Europe

Famous for...

Mussels
Mussels, usually served with fries, is a very popular dish

Lace
Some of the world's finest lace is made in Brussels and Bruges

Diamonds
Antwerp is the center of the world's industrial diamond industry

Saxophone
Invented here in the 1840s

Population:	10.5 million
Money:	**Euro**
Language:	**Flemish**
Hello:	**goede morgen**
Pronunciation:	**khoodemohrg'n**

France

The French landscape includes the mountains of the Pyrenees and Alps, the rocky coastline of Brittany, and the Mediterranean beaches of the southern coast. It is one of the world's leading agricultural countries, producing a wide range of farm products. France is highly industrialized, with oil refining, steel production and chemical processing among its industries. It also has western Europe's second largest car manufacturing industry, mostly based in Paris. The French people have a long tradition of elegance and style and Paris continues to be a world leader in the fashion industry.

The French TGV train carries passengers at up to 186 miles per hour

Lavender, used in perfumes, is grown around Grasse

The long, slim French bread is famous worldwide

The Arc de Triomphe in Paris was built to honor the Emperor Napoleon

A typical tree-lined avenue in the beautiful Rhône Valley, in southern France

The Eiffel Tower in Paris stands at 985 feet high

Calais
Lille
Boulogne
Dieppe
Cherbourg
Seine River
Reims
Metz
PARIS
Strasbourg
Brittany
Orléans
Auxerre
Loire River
Poitiers
Vichy
Lyons
Limoges St. Etienne
Alps
Bordeaux
Garonne River
Rhône River
Nice
Montpelier
Marseille Grasse
Toulouse
Cannes
Pyrenees

Garlic is an important part of French cooking

Much of the French countryside is given over to vineyards

More than 300 types of cheese are made in France

Famous for...

Wine
France produces about a quarter of the world's wine. Champagne is made in the area around Reims

Perfume
Scented grasses and flowers are made into some of the world's finest perfumes

Croissants
Freshly baked breads and pastries are eaten for breakfast

Tour de France
The gruelling, month-long cycling race takes place across France's varied countryside, including steep mountains. People line the streets to cheer the cyclists as they pass through towns and villages

Café culture
The tradition of visiting cafés to eat, drink and meet people began in France in the 17th century. Cafés are now popular all over the world

Film
Moving pictures, projected onto a screen, were invented here by the Lumière brothers in 1895

Film festival
A famous film festival is held each year in Cannes

Population:	61.9 million
Money:	Euro
Language:	French
Hello:	Bonjour
Pronunciation:	bohn-ZHOOR

Italy

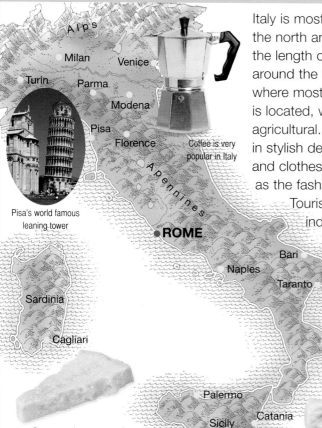

Italy is mostly mountainous, with the Alps in the north and the Apennines running along the length of the country. The northern region, around the cities of Milan and Turin, is where most of the country's industry is located, while the south is mainly agricultural. Italy is a world leader in stylish design, especially for cars and clothes – Milan is widely regarded as the fashion capital of the world. Tourism is a hugely important industry, with millions of tourists coming to visit ancient Roman sites and historic cities such as Venice, Naples and Florence.

Coffee is very popular in Italy

Italy is the home of pizza

Pisa's world famous leaning tower

Parmesan cheese comes from the region around Parma

Positano is a town of brightly colored villas perched on steep cliffs

Pasta, in all its various forms, is one of the world's most popular foods

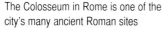

The unique city of Venice is famous for its canals and many historical buildings

The Colosseum in Rome is one of the city's many ancient Roman sites

Famous for...

Wine
Italy has been making wine for thousands of years and is the world's largest wine producer

Ferrari
The world famous sports cars are made in Modena

Art
Some of the world's most important works of art were made by Italian artists such as Michaelangelo and Leonardo da Vinci

Soccer
Italians are passionate about soccer and have some of the best teams in the world

Population:	59 million
Money:	Euro
Language:	Italian
Hello:	Buon giorno
Pronunciation:	bwohn JOR-noh

San Marino

SAN MARINO The tiny Republic of San Marino is built on the steep slopes of Mount Titano and is completely surrounded by Italy. The capital itself is an ancient fortress with steep cobbled streets, and is one of the venues for Grand Prix races.

Population:	31,400
Money:	Euro
Language:	Italian
Hello:	Buon giorno
Pronunciation:	bwohn JOR-noh

Vatican City

The world's smallest independent state is situated in the center of Rome. It is the capital of Roman Catholicism and home to the Pope.

St. Peter's Basilica in Vatican City is one of the most visited religious sites in the world

Population:	900
Money:	Euro
Language:	Italian
Hello:	Buon giorno
Pronunciation:	bwohn JOR-noha

Spain

Spain is the third largest country in Europe and includes the Balearic and Canary Islands. Mountains dominate much of the Spanish landscape, from the Pyrenees on the border with France and the Sierra Nevada in the south, to the Cantabrian Mountains in the northwest. Spain is one of the world's largest producers of olives and olive oil. The olives are harvested by beating the trees with sticks. Fishing is an important industry along the northern coast, and fleets of boats spend months in fishing grounds far from shore.

Oranges and lemons are grown along the east coast

Real Madrid and Barcelona's soccer clubs are among the best teams in the world

Barcelona

Real Madrid

Population:	44.6 million
Money:	Euro
Language:	Spanish
Hello:	Hola
Pronunciation:	oh-lah

The south is the home of the flamenco dance and music

Spicy chorizo sausage is a popular food

Much of the south and east of Spain is taken up by huge olive groves

Andorra

The principality of Andorra lies high in the Pyrenees between France and Spain. Many people visit to go skiing.

Population:	82,000
Money:	Euro
Language:	Catalan
Hello:	Hola
Pronunciation:	oh-lah

Madrid is full of beautiful buildings such as the Palace of Communications

The Sagrada Familia Cathedral is one of the most famous sights in the city of Barcelona

Spain's many sandy beaches attract millions of tourists from all over Europe

Portugal

Portugal has rugged hills in the north, where the climate is cool and rainy. The south is flat with very little rain. Most people live in the north and central regions, where there are forested mountains, deep valleys and rivers. There are many vineyards and groves of olive, almond, fig and orange trees. Fishing is a very important industry, and the largest catch is sardines (the most popular way of eating them is to have them grilled). Other important industries include textile production, winemaking and manufacturing footwear, all of which are exported throughout Europe and the world.

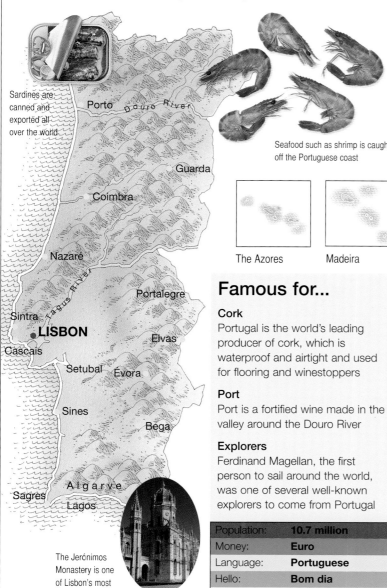

Sardines are canned and exported all over the world

Seafood such as shrimp is caught off the Portuguese coast

The Azores   Madeira

The Jerónimos Monastery is one of Lisbon's most impressive buildings

Famous for...

Cork
Portugal is the world's leading producer of cork, which is waterproof and airtight and used for flooring and winestoppers

Port
Port is a fortified wine made in the valley around the Douro River

Explorers
Ferdinand Magellan, the first person to sail around the world, was one of several well-known explorers to come from Portugal

Population:	**10.7 million**
Money:	**Euro**
Language:	**Portuguese**
Hello:	**Bom dia**
Pronunciation:	**bohn DEE-ah**

Greece

The warm Greek climate is perfect for growing lemons

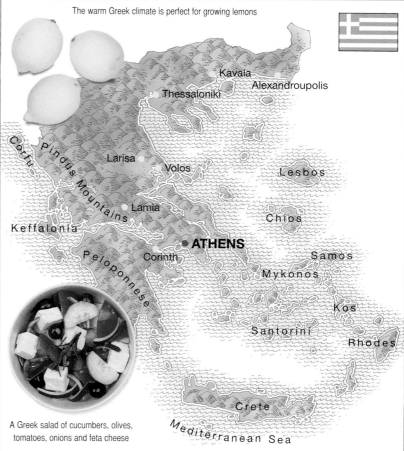

A Greek salad of cucumbers, olives, tomatoes, onions and feta cheese

Greece is made up of a mainland peninsula and 2,000 islands known for their beautiful mountain landscapes and crystal clear waters. The country is surrounded by three seas – the Aegean, the Ionian and the Mediterranean. Ferries are an important means of travel between the many islands and the mainland. Greece has the largest merchant ship fleet in the world. Tourism is a huge industry – tourists come to the island resorts and to visit the ruins of ancient Greece.

Famous for...

Olives
Olives have been grown in Greece for more than 2,000 years

Olympics
The games began in ancient Greece. The first modern Olympics were held in Athens in 1896

Mount Olympus
At 9,750 feet, this is the highest point in Greece. It was thought to be the home of the gods in ancient times

Population:	**11.2 million**
Money:	**Euro**
Language:	**Greek**
Hello:	**Kalimera**
Pronunciation:	**kah-lee-MEH-rah**

Germany

Germany has the largest population in Europe and is the wealthiest country on the continent. There are low plains in the north, rolling forested hills in the center and the Bavarian Alps in the south. The Rhine is Germany's major river, providing a transportation route for cargo across Europe. Germany is a world leader in science and technology, with large exports of cars, electronics and other industrial goods. It has also led the way in producing 'green' products that cause less harm to the environment.

Kiel
Rostock
Lübeck
Hamburg
Bremen
Elbe River
Hanover
BERLIN
Münster
Duisburg
Dortmund
Dusseldorf
Kassel
Leipzig
Cologne
Dresden
Bonn
Erfurt
Frankfurt
Rhine River
Nuremberg
Black Forest
Stuttgart
Bavarian Alps
Munich

Beer is brewed in most major towns and cities

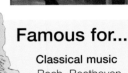

Sausages are a very popular food here

Clear rivers, high mountains and unspoilt woodland are features of the Black Forest

Frankfurt is the business capital. Many international companies have offices here

Germany makes some of the best cars in the world

German bread is heavy and dark in color

There are many beautiful castles in the southern region of Bavaria

A traditional house in the Black Forest, in the southwest of the country

The Brandenburg Gate is at the point that divided east and west Berlin

Famous for...

Classical music
Bach, Beethoven and Wagner are among the great German classical music composers

Electrical goods
Germany leads the world in the production of large electrical goods such as washing machines

Berlin Wall
Germany was once divided between east and west. The wall across the capital that symbolized the divide was torn down in 1989

Cakes
Chocolate and fruit cakes made in Germany are popular all over the world

Population:	82.5 million
Money:	Euro
Language:	German
Hello:	Guten Tag
Pronunciation:	GOOT-en tahk

Austria

Majestic mountains and deep valleys in the south and west of Austria make up 70% of the country. Ibex (mountain goat) and chamois (antelope) can be found here. Austria is one of Europe's most heavily wooded countries, with forests of oak, beech and conifer. At 6,500 feet the trees give way to mountain meadows. Mountain rivers generate hydroelectric power for much of the country.

The Hohensalzburg Fortress in Salzburg is the largest of its kind in Europe

Tourists go hiking in the Austrian Alps in the summer and skiing in the winter

The lakeside village of Hallstatt is one of the oldest in Austria

Famous for...

Vienna Boys Choir
For 500 years the Choir has been known for its beautiful singing

Lipizzaner horses
These pure white horses perform in a special show in Vienna

Composers
Mozart, Haydn, Schubert and the Strauss family come from Austria

Graphite
Mined here, it is used to make the lead in pencils

Population:	**8.4 million**
Money:	**Euro**
Language:	**German**
Hello:	**Guten Tag**
Pronunciation:	**GOOT-en tahk**

Switzerland

The Alps dominate Switzerland, making up over 60% of the land. The highest mountain is Monte Rosa at 15,203 feet, although the better known Matterhorn and Eiger are more spectacular. Heavy winter snows in the mountains make it one of Europe's top skiing destinations. Banking and other financial services are very important to the economy, as is the manufacture of small, precisely engineered items such as clocks and watches.

Zurich
Neucahtel
Lucerne
BERN
Lausanne
▲ Eiger
Montreux
Geneva
▲ Matterhorn

Zurich is Switzerland's most populated city and is its cultural capital

Mountaineers from all over the world take up the challenge of climbing the Matterhorn

Lucerne is a pretty town, popular with tourists exploring the lakes and mountains

The first milk chocolate was invented in Switzerland in 1875

Famous for...

Skiing
Many of the world's top skiers are Swiss

Red Cross
This international aid agency was set up in Switzerland in 1863

Swiss army knife
This consists of many blades and implements that can be folded down into the handle

Watches and clocks
Swiss clocks are known for their accuracy

Population:	**7.5 million**
Money:	**Swiss franc**
Language:	**French**
Hello:	**Bonjour**
Pronunciation:	**bohn-ZHOOR**

Poland

Poland's flat land is perfect for growing crops. To the south the land gets hillier, and beneath the hills of Katowice lies one of the world's largest coal fields. Coal provides energy for the iron and steel mills which in turn provide the metal for Poland's many machine-building factories. Storks are a familiar sight in many Polish villages. They build their nests on roofs and chimneys.

The Old Town in Warsaw was completely rebuilt after the Second World War

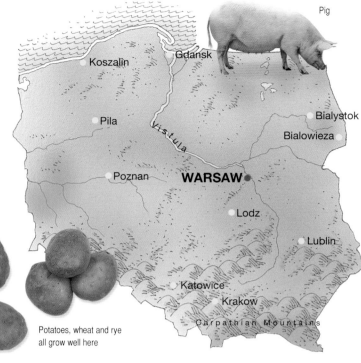
Pig

Koszalin
Gdansk
Pila
Bialystok
Vistula
Bialowieza
Poznan
WARSAW
Lodz
Lublin
Katowice
Krakow
Carpathian Mountains

Potatoes, wheat and rye all grow well here

Famous for...

Salt pork
Used in many traditional dishes

Bigos
'Hunter's stew' is a favorite, filling meal

Vodka
The national alcoholic drink

Bison
European bison can be found in Bialowieza National Park

Zinc
Mined in the south of the country, it is used in batteries

Population:	38 million
Money:	Zloty
Language:	Polish
Hello:	Czesc
Pronunciation:	chesht

Czech Republic

This popular tourist destination has warm summers and cold, snowy winters. The different styles of buildings in the capital, Prague, have made it one of Europe's most beautiful cities. The Czech region of Bohemia is famous for glassmaking. Glass is made by melting sand, soda and limestone. It is then painted, engraved or cut into intricate designs. The glassmakers produce jewelry and stained glass windows as well as fine drinking glasses.

Liberec
PRAGUE
Kolin
Pardubice
Plzen
Svitavy
Brno
Budejovice
Breclav

Týn Church in Prague in winter

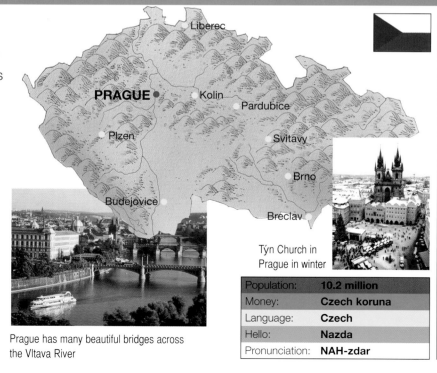
Prague has many beautiful bridges across the Vltava River

Population:	10.2 million
Money:	Czech koruna
Language:	Czech
Hello:	Nazda
Pronunciation:	NAH-zdar

Slovakia

The High Tatras mountain range is popular for skiing, and is also home to wolves, lynxes, chamois and mink. Slovaks are proud of their traditional dress and music.

Zilina
Kosice
BRATISLAVA

Population:	5.4 million
Money:	Euro
Language:	Slovak
Hello:	Nazdar
Pronunciation:	NAH-zdar

Belarus

Belarus has the largest marshlands in Europe and forests of silver birch, pine, oak and beech which provide timber for building and papermaking. Mushroom picking is popular. Any mushrooms that are not eaten immediately are dried, salted or pickled for use throughout the winter.

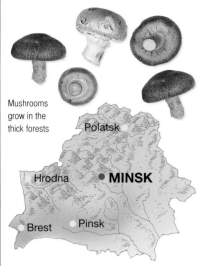

Mushrooms grow in the thick forests

MINSK
Polatsk
Hrodna
Brest   Pinsk

Some of the more remote and untouched forests are home to wild elks

Population:	9.7 million
Money:	Belarussian rouble
Language:	Belarussian
Hello:	Pryvitannie
Pronunciation:	pri-VEET-an-nyyeh

Ukraine

KIEV
Kharkiv
Dnipro
Odessa   Donetsk

Ukraine is a center of sugar production

Ukraine is one of the most fertile places on earth. Huge quantities of wheat, rye, oats and sugar beet are grown on the country's vast, rolling plains. Beneath the rich, black soil lie other treasures – coal and metal ores. The coal provides energy for Ukraine's iron, steel and machine-building industries. The Donbass Basin is Europe's largest coalfield.

St Andrew's Church in Kiev is topped with five spectacular domes

Population:	45.9 million
Money:	Hryvnya
Language:	Ukrainian
Hello:	Pryvit
Pronunciation:	pri-veet

Hungary

Budapest is the lively capital city

Hot summers and mild winters make Hungary suitable for growing many crops. Almost half of the world's paprika comes from here. Budapest is actually two cities, Buda and Pest, which lie on either side of the Danube River.

Danube
BUDAPEST
Lake Balaton
Pécs   Szeged

Famous for...

Goulash
Beef and vegetable stew spiced with paprika

Holograms
Invented by the Hungarian Denis Gabor. He received the Nobel Prize in 1971

Paprika
A spice that is grown here

Population:	10 million
Money:	Forint
Language:	Hungarian
Hello:	Szia
Pronunciation:	ZEE-yah

Romania

Botosani
Timisoara   Brasov
BUCHAREST

This land of fairytale castles, medieval cities and mountain forests is also one of the poorest in Europe. Most people work on farms and many still travel by horse and cart. Many Roma (gypsies) live here, and these nomadic people have a long tradition of horse-training, music and acrobatics. The legend of Count Dracula is based on Vlad the Impaler, who was born in the medieval town of Sighisoara.

Home-grown fruits and vegetables can be found in many small markets

Population:	21.3 million
Money:	Romanian leu
Language:	Romanian
Hello:	Buna ziua
Pronunciation:	BOO-nuh ZEE-wa

Bulgaria

Rose petals are sent to distilleries to make attar

Bulgaria is popular with tourists, who come for the dramatic mountains, golden beaches and ancient Roman ruins. Bulgaria's healthy climate, clear warm seas and mineral springs are thought to cure many illnesses. Roses are grown to make attar, an oil used in perfume.

Vineyards thrive in Bulgaria's climate, and red wine is exported around the world

Population:	7.6 million
Money:	Lev
Language:	Bulgarian
Hello:	Dobur Den
Pronunciation:	dob-ur den

Serbia

Serbia became a republic in 2006, after Montenegro voted for independence from the Union of Serbia and Montenegro. Kosovo is an area within Serbia controlled by the United Nations.

Population:	9.9 million
Money:	Divar
Language:	Serbian
Hello:	Zdravo
Pronunciation:	zdrah-voh

Montenegro

Montenegro became its own state in 2006. White-water rafting on the Tara River is a popular pastime.

Population:	598,000
Money:	Euro
Language:	Serbian/Montenegrin
Hello:	Zdravo
Pronunciation:	zdrah-voh

Slovenia

Slovenia is a hilly country covered in forest. Hiking and skiing in the mountains are popular. There are some very deep caves beneath its mountains, and many unique animals can be found here.

Population:	2 million
Money:	Euro
Language:	Slovene
Hello:	Zivjo
Pronunciation:	zhee-vee-yo

Bosnia
and Herzegovina

This country has beautiful lakes and forests. The population is made up of three groups: the Serbs, Croats and Bosnian Muslims.

Population:	4 million
Money:	Convertible mark
Language:	Bosnian
Hello:	Zdravo
Pronunciation:	zdrah-voh

Croatia

Many people visit Croatia's beautiful Adriatic coast and its 1,185 islands. Split has one of the finest Roman ruins in the world – a palace built in 295 AD.

Dalmatians were first bred here

Population:	4.6 million
Money:	Kuna
Language:	Croatian
Hello:	Zdarvo
Pronunciation:	ZDRAD-vo

Macedonia

This green and beautiful land experiences frequent earth tremors and earthquakes. Tobacco is Macedonia's main crop.

Tobacco

Population:	2 million
Money:	Macedonian denar
Language:	Macedonian
Hello:	Prijatno
Pronunciation:	pree-yat-no

Moldova

Sunflowers and grapes grow well in the mild climate

Cereal, vegetables and fruit are important exports, while oil is a major import. Carpet weaving has been an art form here for centuries.

Population:	3.8 million
Money:	Moldovan leu
Language:	Moldovan
Hello:	Buna ziua
Pronunciation:	BOO-nuh ZEE-wa

Cyprus

There are many ancient ruins and castles on Cyprus. Greek Cypriots live in the southern part of the island while Turkish Cypriots live in the north.

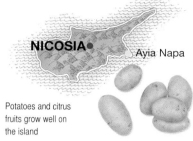

Potatoes and citrus fruits grow well on the island

Population:	863,000
Money:	Euro
Language:	Greek, Turkish
Hello:	Kalimera
Pronunciation:	kah-lee-MEH-rah

Turkey

Turkey is a land of rocky coastlines, grassy plains, mountains and fertile valleys. Flocks of sheep are raised on the central plains to produce lamb's wool for making Turkey's famous carpets. Angora goats, from Ankara, have long wavy hair which is used to make mohair. Cotton, grown in western Turkey, is used by American and European fashion designers.

Lamb's wool is soft and strong

Nuts and dried fruit are a popular snack here

Famous for...

Shish kebabs
The Turkish way of grilling lamb on skewers

Turkish delight
A sweet made from sugar and gum

Belly dancing
An ancient fertility dance still popular at Turkish weddings

Turkish rugs
Good quality carpets, noted for being colorful and stylish

Turkish baths
Half an hour in hot steam followed by body brushing, dousing in cold water and then a relaxing massage

Istanbul's Grand Covered Bazaar is a maze of streets with over 3,000 shops

Turkey's position between Asia and Europe has led to a mix of architectural styles

Population:	75.8 million
Money:	Turkish lira
Language:	Turkish
Hello:	Merhaba
Pronunciation:	MARE-huh-buh

Albania

Albania has rugged mountains and beautiful beaches, where rare Dalmatian pelicans can be seen. Summers here are hot and dry. The economy is mainly agricultural.

Population:	3.2 million
Money:	Lek
Language:	Albanian
Hello:	Mire dite
Pronunciation:	meer-dee-tah

Malta

The rocky island of Malta has some of the oldest buildings in the world. There are many religious festivals celebrated with music, fireworks and processions.

Nougat is eaten at festivals

Population:	408,000
Money:	Euro
Language:	Maltese
Hello:	Merhba
Pronunciation:	mehr-hah-bah

Russian Federation

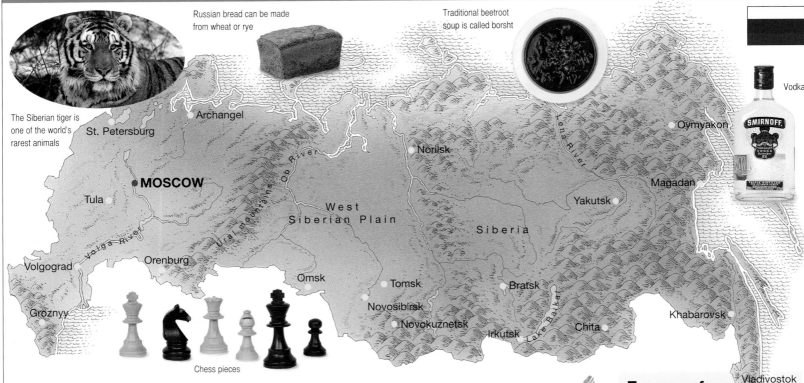

The Siberian tiger is one of the world's rarest animals

Russian bread can be made from wheat or rye

Traditional beetroot soup is called borsht

Vodka

Chess pieces

Russia is the largest country on earth (about 6,000 miles wide), and it spans 11 time zones. Kalingrad is a part of Russia, but is separated from the rest of the country by Lithuania and Latvia. The Ural Mountains divide Russia: to the west, the country is in Europe, to the east it is in Asia. 80% of the population live in the European part of Russia. The Trans-Siberian Railway links Moscow in the west and Vladivostok in the east, and it takes six days to travel between the two. The railway is vital for trade and communication. Much of Russia is empty grassland or forest, and Siberia has the largest forest in the world – home to elk, brown bear and sable. Russia also has the world's deepest lake, Lake Baikal, which contains one quarter of the world's fresh water.

The ballet schools in St. Petersburg and Moscow are world famous

Famous for...

Space exploration
Yuri Gagarin was the first person in space. He orbited the Earth in 1961

Caviar
These fish eggs are considered a great delicacy and are served on buckwheat pancakes

Chess
Many of the world's greatest chess players have been Russian

Vodka
A strong alcoholic liquor made by distilling grain or potatoes

Ballet
Enjoyed by people of all ages

Population:	**142.8 million**
Money:	**Russian rouble**
Language:	**Russian**
Hello:	**Zdravstvuite**
Pronunciation:	**zzDRAST-vet-yah**

Russian Orthodox churches, like St. Basil's Cathedral, have onion-shaped domes

The brown bear, found all over Russia, is the country's national symbol

Catherine's Palace in Pushkin, near St. Petersburg, is one of Russia's finest buildings

Kazakhstan

High, grassy plains cover most of the country, with mountains in the east. Gerbils come from the sandy deserts in the south – they are much bigger than those kept as pets.

● ASTANA

Alma Ata

Population:	**15.5 million**
Money:	**Tenge**
Language:	**Kazakh**
Hello:	**Salom**
Pronunciation:	**sah-LAHM**

Uzbekistan

Aral Sea

TASHKENT ●

Bukhoro

The inland Aral Sea is shrinking due to water taken for cotton crops. It has lost 75% of its water, changing the local climate. Cotton is one of the largest exports.

Population:	**27.8 million**
Money:	**Som**
Language:	**Uzbek**
Hello:	**Salaam a'alaykum**
Pronunciation:	**sah-LAHM ah ah-LAY-koom**

Kyrgyzstan

Much of this high, mountainous country is under permanent snow, but Lake Issyk-Kul is slightly salty and never freezes. Snow leopards are found in the wild.

BISHKEK ● Lake Issyk-Kul

Osh

Snow leopard

Population:	**5.4 million**
Money:	**Som**
Language:	**Kyrgyz**
Hello:	**Salaam**
Pronunciation:	**sah-LAHM**

Tajikistan

DUSHANBE

Pamir mountains

Tajikistan experiences both winter snow storms and summer dust storms. Wolves live on the lower parts of the mountain ranges.

Wolf

Population:	**6.8 million**
Money:	**Somoni**
Language:	**Tajik**
Hello:	**Salom**
Pronunciation:	**sah-LOM**

Georgia

With its beaches, snow-covered mountains and grassy plains full of flowers, Georgia is a popular holiday destination.

Lemons, limes and apricots are grown here

Gagra

● TBILISI

Population:	**4.4 million**
Money:	**Lari**
Language:	**Georgian**
Hello:	**Gamarjobet**
Pronunciation:	**gah-mar-joh-baht**

Armenia

Gymuri

Lake Sevan

● **YEREVAN**

Walnuts

Armenia is a mountainous land of hot, dusty summers and cold, dry winters. Earthquakes are a danger and can destroy towns. A popular snack is a string of walnuts covered in sticky grape juice.

Population:	**3 million**
Money:	**Dram**
Language:	**Armenian**
Hello:	**Parev**
Pronunciation:	**bar-ev**

Turkmenistan

Turkmenistan has very few inhabitants for its size, due to four-fifths of the land being inhospitable desert. In the Kugitang Mountains you can see dinosaur footprints.

Turkmenbashi

Kugitang ● **ASHGABAT**

Population:	**5 million**
Money:	**Manat**
Language:	**Turkmen**
Hello:	**Salaam**
Pronunciation:	**sah-LAHM**

Azerbaijan

This small country has been exporting oil for many years. The first-ever oil pipeline was built here – it was made of wood.

Yevlakh **BAKU** ●

Population:	**8.5 million**
Money:	**Manat**
Language:	**Azerbaijani**
Hello:	**Salam**
Pronunciation:	**sah-LAHM**

Iran

Iran is a mountainous country with active volcanoes, and earthquakes are a natural hazard. It is very windy – summer winds can reach up to 70 miles per hour. The country has a huge salt waste (200 miles long) which is unexplored due to the treacherous terrain. Iran is famous for its carpets, made here since the 5th century BC.

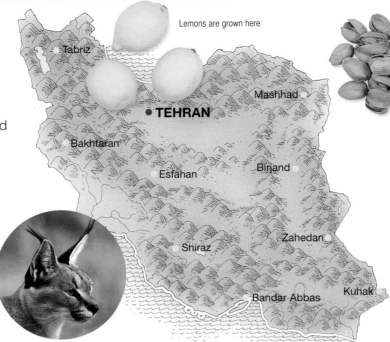

Lemons are grown here

Tabriz

Mashhad

● TEHRAN

Bakhtaran

Esfahan

Birjand

Shiraz

Zahedan

Bandar Abbas

Kuhak

Pistachio nuts are a major Iranian crop

The citadel, part of the huge mud city of Bam, in southeastern Iran

Wild cats live in Iran's deserts and mountains

Women in Iran wearing a traditional Islamic dress called a burkha

Population:	72.2 million
Money:	Iranian rial
Language:	Farsi
Hello:	Sa'lem
Pronunciation:	sah-LEM

Israel

Israel is a small country which has fertile valleys, beautiful beaches, dusty deserts and rolling hills. It has influenced every corner of the world since it is the Holy Land for Jews, Christians and Muslims. Only 25% of the people living in Israel were born there. The rest come from over 100 different countries, so signs in shops are often in many different languages.

Nazareth

West Bank

Tel Aviv

JERUSALEM ●

Gaza Strip

Dead Sea

Eilat

Oranges are grown here and exported all over the world

The Dome of the Rock Mosque, on Temple Mount in the city of Jerusalem

Famous for...

Dead Sea
This is the lowest body of water on Earth, and it has eight times more salt in it than the oceans – you can float on its surface

Jewish holy sites
Tourists from all over the world travel here to see sites such as the Wailing Wall and the remains of Solomon's Temple

Population:	7 million
Money:	Shekel
Language:	Hebrew
Hello:	Shalom
Pronunciation:	sha-LOHM

Palestine

There are two areas within Israel that are run by the Palestinians. They would like the West Bank and the Gaza Strip to be recognized as a separate country.

West Bank

Jericho

JERUSALEM ●

Bethlehem

Gaza

Gaza Strip

Population:	4 million
Money:	Jordanian dinar
Language:	Arabic
Hello:	Salaam a'alaykum
Pronunciation:	sah-LAHM ah ah-LAY-koom

Iraq

Most of Iraq is desert, but two main rivers, the Tigris and the Euphrates, flow through the country. The area between these rivers (known as Mesopotamia) was home to the first civilizations to develop in human history. It was here people first lived in towns and developed writing and, according to the Bible, the Garden of Eden was said to exist here. Today, the fertile land is used to grow dates and cotton. The country is one of the world's largest producers of dates.

Mosul
Kirkuk
Tigris
Euphrates
BAGHDAD
Fresh dates
Karbala
An Najaf
Basra

The Iraqi capital, Baghdad, has many old mosques and other sacred buildings

Date palms grow in the fertile valleys alongside the Tigris and Euphrates Rivers

Population:	29.5 million
Money:	Iraqi dinar
Language:	Arabic
Hello:	Salaam a'alaykum
Pronunciation:	sah-LAHM ah ah-LAY-koom

Kuwait

Kuwait has a flat, gravelly desert. Water has to be pumped from deep in the ground or taken from the sea. The seawater has to go through a process to make it suitable for drinking or watering crops.

Al Bahrah
KUWAIT CITY
Fresh water is a precious liquid
Al Wafra

Population:	2.9 million
Money:	Kuwaiti dinar
Language:	Arabic
Hello:	Salaam a'alaykum
Pronunciation:	sah-LAHM ah ah-LAY-koom

Saudi Arabia

Saudi Arabia is a dry, desert land, ruled by the Saud Ibn Saud family. It has a quarter of the world's oil reserves which has made the country very wealthy. Mohammed, the founder of the religion of Islam, was born in Mecca, and every year around 2 million Muslim pilgrims travel to this holy place. Over 20,000 buses are needed to transport the pilgrims around the country.

Al Jawf
Tabuk
Dammam
Medina
RIYADH
Jedda
Layla
Mecca
Najran

The Muslim pilgrimage to Mecca is the world's largest annual religious gathering

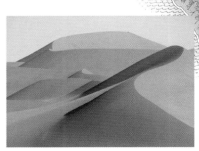

Much of Saudi Arabia is covered with vast desert sand dunes

Population:	25.2 million
Money:	Saudi riyal
Language:	Arabic
Hello:	Salaam a'alaykum
Pronunciation:	sah-LAHM ah ah-LAY-koom

Qatar

Al Khawr
DOHA

Qatar is a very flat country, with gravelly desert and very little vegetation. In summer, temperatures can reach up to 122° Fahrenheit. It is also very humid, and the country suffers from sandstorms.

Population:	855,000
Money:	Qatari riyal
Language:	Arabic
Hello:	Salaam a'alaykum
Pronunciation:	sah-LAHM ah ah-LAY-koom

Syria

Historically, Syria was on a key trading route, and was therefore invaded many times. Today you can see the ruins left by the various empires – one of the most famous is the Roman city of Palmyra. The world's first alphabet was developed at Ugarit. Desert sandstorms are a natural hazard.

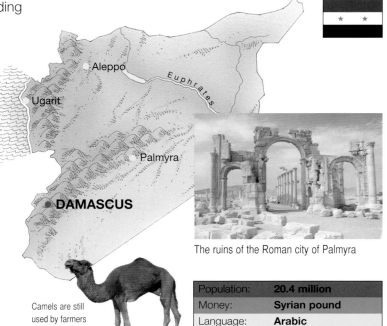

The dome of the Sayyida Ruqayya Mosque in the Syrian capital, Damascus

The ruins of the Roman city of Palmyra

Camels are still used by farmers for farm work and pulling carts to market

Population:	20.4 million
Money:	Syrian pound
Language:	Arabic
Hello:	Salaam a'alaykum
Pronunciation:	sah-LAHM ah ah-LAY-koom

United Arab Emirates (U.A.E)

The United Arab Emirates is divided into seven regions, each ruled by a sheik. The discovery of oil has made this an incredibly wealthy area.

Population:	4.5 million
Money:	UAE dirham
Language:	Arabic
Hello:	Salaam a'alaykum
Pronunciation:	sah-LAHM ah ah-LAY-koom

Jordan

Goats grazing in the desert

Jordan's desert is part of the huge Syrian Desert

The pink city of Petra was carved into solid rock 2,000 years ago

Most of Jordan is desert, and there are few trees and not much farmland. The Jordan River is considered a holy river by Christians, and many churches buy water from it to use at christenings. Tourists come here to see the old Biblical cities of the Jordan River valley and the ruins of the ancient city of Petra, whose magnificent buildings and tombs were carved out of red sandstone cliffs.

Population:	6.1 million
Money:	Jordanian dinar
Language:	Arabic
Hello:	Salaam a'alaykum
Pronunciation:	sah-LAHM ah ah-LAY-koom

Afghanistan

Afghanistan has few railways or roads, and the rivers are not suitable for boats, so pack animals transport goods through the fertile valleys, over the mountains and across desert plains. Most Afghans are farmers, growing just enough fruit, vegetables and cereals to feed their families.

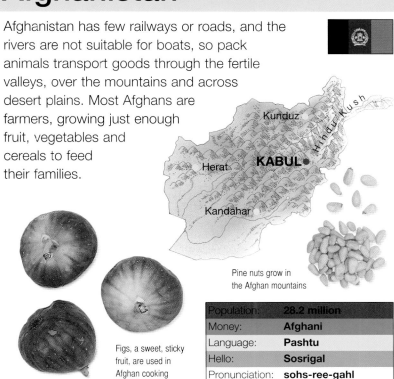

Pine nuts grow in the Afghan mountains

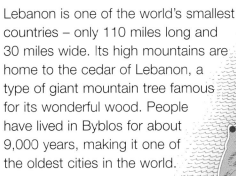

Figs, a sweet, sticky fruit, are used in Afghan cooking

Population:	28.2 million
Money:	Afghani
Language:	Pashtu
Hello:	Sosrigal
Pronunciation:	sohs-ree-gahl

Lebanon

Lebanon is one of the world's smallest countries – only 110 miles long and 30 miles wide. Its high mountains are home to the cedar of Lebanon, a type of giant mountain tree famous for its wonderful wood. People have lived in Byblos for about 9,000 years, making it one of the oldest cities in the world.

A tasty snack of hummus and falafel

Golden and Imperial eagles live in the mountains of Lebanon

Population:	4.1 million
Money:	Lebanese pound
Language:	Arabic
Hello:	Salaam a'alaykum
Pronunciation:	sah-LAHM ah ah-LAY-koom

Yemen

Yemen is mostly desert – hot and dry in the east, hot and humid along the coast. Since it has virtually no fresh water, the people depend on water from oases. Dried and salted fish is an important export.

Population:	23 million
Money:	Yemeni rial
Language:	Arabic
Hello:	Salaam a'alaykum
Pronunciation:	sah-LAHM ah ah-LAY-koom

Oman

Oman is ruled by a sultan, and its main export is oil. Dates, limes and nuts are grown. Many rare animals live in Oman, including the giant sea turtle which can grow up to 9 feet in length.

Dates

Population:	2.6 million
Money:	Omani rial
Language:	Arabic
Hello:	Salaam a'alaykum
Pronunciation:	sah-LAHM ah ah-LAY-koom

Bahrain

Bahrain is a group of 34 islands. Much of its money comes from oil refining, and most food is imported.

Many wading birds, such as the greater flamingo, live in the shallow waters around the islands

Population:	766,000
Money:	Bahraini dinar
Language:	Arabic
Hello:	Salaam a'alaykum
Pronunciation:	sah-LAHM ah ah-LAY-koom

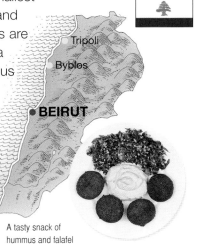

India

India is a huge country with the second largest population in the world. The mixture of peoples and religions means that more than 24 languages are spoken. India is full of variety – from bustling cities to remote farming villages, and from snow-capped mountains to vast forests and hot plains. Most of India has three seasons in a year – hot, wet and cool. The Ganges is the sacred river of the Hindus. It is a source of food, means of travel and transport, people wash laundry and bathe in it, and the dead are cremated along its banks.

Over 9 million people live in Mumbai, making it one of the largest cities in the world

The Taj Mahal is India's most famous building. It took 20,000 people to build it

India's national animal, the tiger, can still be found in some dense forests, although it is endangered

Hot, spicy chilis are a common ingredient in Indian cooking

India is the largest tea producer in the world

Nepal

Tourists come to Nepal to see Mount Everest. Many herbs used in medicines are found on the slopes of Nepal's mountains.

KATHMANDU • ▲ Mt. Everest

At 29,028 feet high, Mount Everest is the tallest mountain in the world

Population:	28.8 million
Money:	Nepalese rupee
Language:	Nepali
Hello:	Namaste
Pronunciation:	nah-mah-STAY

Map Labels

NEW DELHI
Jaipur
Kanpur
Varanasi
Ganges
Vadodara
Bhopal
Surat
Nagpur
Kolkata (Calcutta)
Mumbai (Bombay)
Vishakhapatnam
Hyderabad
Chennai (Madras)
Bangalore
Arabian Sea
Indian Ocean
Imphal
Himalayas

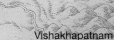

Andaman Islands

Nicobar Islands

Famous for...

Cricket
India's cricket team is respected all over the world

Temples
There are many beautifully carved Hindu, Sikh and Jain temples

Sacred cows
Cows are sacred in India – you'll see them everywhere!

Bollywood
Mumbai is home to the 'Bollywood' film industry. More films are made here than in Hollywood. They attract large audiences and the actors are huge stars

Curry
Everyone eats curry, even for breakfast!

Population:	1.2 billion
Money:	Indian rupee
Language:	Hindi
Hello:	Namaste
Pronunciation:	nah-mah-STAY

Pakistan

Pakistan is a dry country with rocky deserts and huge mountains (including K2, the second highest in the world). Most people live near the Indus River where they can grow crops. Pakistan grows a lot of cotton, and the cotton seeds are picked by hand. Raw cotton is exported, as well as cotton thread, fabric and clothes.

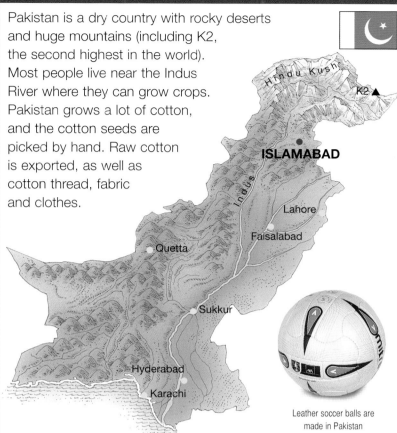

Leather soccer balls are made in Pakistan

Pakistani drivers like to decorate their vehicles in bright colors

K2, regarded as one of the world's hardest mountains to climb, is in northern Pakistan

Population:	167 million
Money:	Pakistani rupee
Language:	Urdu
Hello:	Salaam
Pronunciation:	sah-LAHM

Bangladesh

Bangladesh often experiences terrible floods because of its huge rivers and flat land. The plains are perfect for growing rice.

Population:	161.3 million
Money:	Taka
Language:	Bengali
Hello:	Kamon achho
Pronunciation:	kay-mohn-ach-hoh

Bhutan

The name Bhutan means 'Thunder Dragon', after the storms that come off the Himalayas. The people keep yaks for their meat and milk, and their dung is also used as fuel.

Population:	666,900
Money:	Ngultrum
Language:	Dzongkha
Hello:	Kuzug zangpo
Pronunciation:	koo-zoog-jahng-poh

Sri Lanka

Over 300,000 tons of tea are produced here every year. Known as the 'Island of Gems', precious stones are mined, cut and made into jewelry.

Elephants are popular with tourists

Population:	19.4 million
Money:	Sri Lanka rupee
Language:	Sinhala
Hello:	Ayubowan
Pronunciation:	ah-you-bo-wahng

Maldives

Reefs teeming with brightly colored fish attract tourists. Global warming is a real hazard, as no island is higher than 6 feet above sea level.

Tourists come here for the white, sandy beaches

Population:	311,100
Money:	Rufiyaa
Language:	Dhivehi
Hello:	Salaam a'aalaykum
Pronunciation:	sah-LAHM ah ah-LAY-koom

Burma

This very hot, tropical country has many natural resources, such as timber and precious stones. Its rubies are considered to be the finest in the world. Sugarcane juice is a popular drink here.

Rubies are mined in Burma

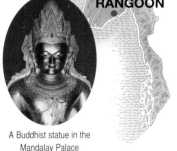

RANGOON

A Buddhist statue in the Mandalay Palace

The Htilominlo Buddhist Temple in Bagan is one of many throughout Burma

Population:	49.2 million
Money:	Kyat
Language:	Burmese
Hello:	Mingalar pa
Pronunciation:	ming-a-lah pa

Laos

The huge Mekong River is the main route through the mountains and forests. Water buffalo are used for heavy farm work and provide milk and meat. Coffee, tea and rice are grown on mountain plateaus.

Luang Prabang
Pak Lai
VIENTIANE
Rice
Mukdahan

Population:	6 million
Money:	New kip
Language:	Lao
Hello:	Sabai dee
Pronunciation:	sah-bie-dee

Cambodia

Most Cambodians live by the huge Mekong River which often floods, making the soil perfect for growing rice.

Angkor
Mekong
PHNOM PENH

Population:	14.7 million
Money:	Riel
Language:	Khmer
Hello:	Jimripsu
Pronunciation:	jihm-rihp-soo-ah

Thailand

Thailand is a hot and humid country, covered in forests and paddy fields.

Tantalum, produced in Thailand, is used in game consoles, cell phones and laptop computers. There are 1,000 different species of butterfly in Thailand. One of the most beautiful is the Golden Birdwing butterfly.

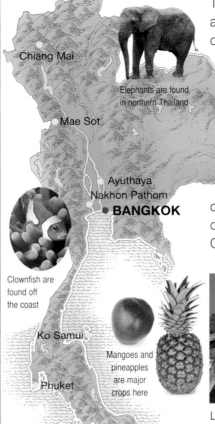

Chiang Mai
Mae Sot
Elephants are found in northern Thailand
Ayuthaya
Nakhon Pathom
BANGKOK
Clownfish are found off the coast
Ko Samui
Mangoes and pineapples are major crops here
Phuket

Longtail boats are used for fishing and diving and as ferries in the seas around Thailand

These women are making flower garlands. They are displayed during religious festivals

Many tourists come to Thailand for the beautiful scenery and great beaches

Famous for...

Tuk-tuks
These motorized rickshaws are perfect for traveling through busy cities

Thai food
Spicy and distinctive, usually featuring garlic, chili, lime and coconut

Temples
There are many beautiful Buddhist temples throughout the country

Population:	64.3 million
Money:	Baht
Language:	Thai
Hello:	Sawatdi khap
Pronunciation:	sa-wa-DEE Krab

Malaysia

Malaysia's dense rainforest has many species of plants and animals, including the world's largest and smelliest flower, the rafflesia flower. Some plants are used by drug companies to make medicines. The largest export is computer chips, used in electronic goods. Kite flying is a popular pastime.

Malay

KUALA LUMPUR

Mersing

Johor Baharu

Sabah

Miri

Bintulu

Sarawak

Kuching

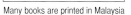

My Big Animal Book

Many books are printed in Malaysia

For many years the Petronas Towers were the world's tallest buildings (1,483 feet high)

Latex from the rubber tree is used to make tires and keypads for remote controls

Population:	**27 million**
Money:	**Ringgit**
Language:	**Malay**
Hello:	**Selamet pagi**
Pronunciation:	**seh-LA-maht PAH-gee**

Singapore

Singapore is a tiny, wealthy country with a busy port. It is one of the most crowded countries in the world, but it is also very clean. Anyone who drops litter must pay a large fine.

Changi

SINGAPORE CITY

Population:	**4.5 million**
Money:	**Singapore dollar**
Language:	**Chinese**
Hello:	**Ni hao**
Pronunciation:	**nee haOW**

Indonesia

Indonesia is made up of 17,000 islands with soaring mountains, dense jungles, white, sandy beaches and active volcanoes. It is the largest group of islands in the world and stretches 3,100 miles from the Indian Ocean to the Pacific Ocean. Indonesia is also the world's largest Muslim country and there are more than 580 different languages spoken here. The climate is ideal for growing all sorts of exotic, tasty fruit, including the thorny durian, which smells horrible but tastes delicious.

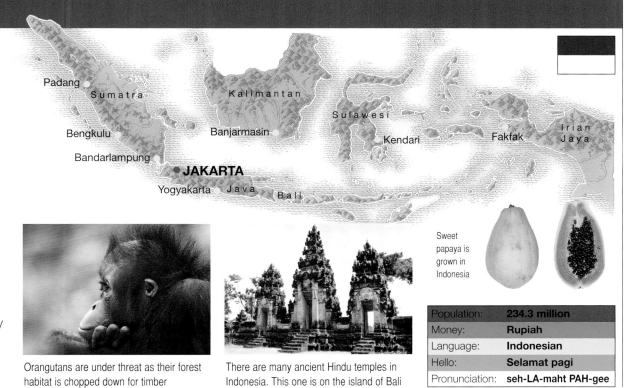

Padang

Sumatra

Kalimantan

Sulawesi

Bengkulu

Banjarmasin

Kendari

Fakfak

Irian Jaya

Bandarlampung

JAKARTA

Yogyakarta   Java

Bali

Sweet papaya is grown in Indonesia

Orangutans are under threat as their forest habitat is chopped down for timber

There are many ancient Hindu temples in Indonesia. This one is on the island of Bali

Population:	**234.3 million**
Money:	**Rupiah**
Language:	**Indonesian**
Hello:	**Selamat pagi**
Pronunciation:	**seh-LA-maht PAH-gee**

Vietnam

Vietnam's large flood plains and hot, wet climate make it an ideal place to grow rice. This is planted by hand in specially flooded paddy fields. Vietnam's many rivers and canals provide fish to eat, water for crops and a means to get around. Boats come in all shapes and sizes – some long and thin, others completely round. In the cities, cyclos are a useful means of getting around. These are pedal powered machines that can transport a whole family.

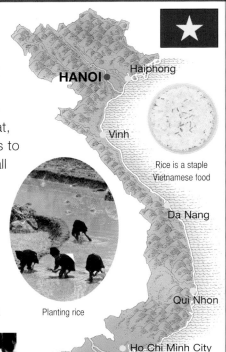

HANOI

Haiphong

Vinh

Da Nang

Qui Nhon

Ho Chi Minh City

Rice is a staple Vietnamese food

Planting rice

Market traders load their bicycles with fruit and other goods for sale

Population:	88.5 million
Money:	Dong
Language:	Vietnamese
Hello:	chao
Pronunciation:	chow

Philippines

The Philippines suffers frequent natural disasters such as floods, earthquakes, typhoons and volcanic eruptions. Traditional houses are on stilts to protect families from flooding and wild animals. The Rice Research Institute in Manila breeds new species of rice to help farmers grow more using less land and less water.

The Philippines is a group of 7,107 islands

Luzon

Dagupan

MANILA

Rattan baskets are made here

Samar

Tacloban

Panay

Bacolod

Palawan

Mindanao

Zamboanga

General Santos

Filipinos living near an active volcano leave their houses as soon as a warning is given

Population:	89.7 million
Money:	Philippine peso
Language:	English
Hello:	Hello
Pronunciation:	hel-lo

East Timor

East Timor is one of the world's newest countries – it became independent from Indonesia in 2002. Coffee is the country's largest export, but deposits of oil and gas have been found offshore.

Tutuala

DILI

Coffee beans

Population:	1.2 million
Money:	US dollar
Language:	Portuguese
Hello:	Bom dia
Pronunciation:	bohn DEE-ah

Brunei

BANDAR SERI BEGAWAN

Tutong

Kampong Sukang

Brunei is a tiny Muslim country ruled by a sultan. Its huge reserves of oil and gas have made both the country and the sultan very wealthy.

The Omar Ali Saifuddin Mosque in Bandar Seri Begawan

Population:	398,000
Money:	Bruneian dollar
Language:	Malay
Hello:	Selemat pagi
Pronunciation:	seh-LA-maht PAH-gee

China

This enormous country is the third largest in the world, and is home to more people than any other country on Earth – one-fifth of the world's population is Chinese. The landscape is very varied, with high mountains in the west and plains in the east, forests in the north, deserts in the center and rainforests in the south. Many places in China have extremes of temperature – very hot in summer and very cold in winter. Over half of the population grow grain, rice and other important crops. Chinese people from different regions speak different dialects but can all understand the written Chinese language. Instead of an alphabet of different letters, each Chinese word has its own character.

Population:	1.34 billion
Money:	Renminbi
Language:	Chinese
Hello:	Ni hao
Pronunciation:	nee haOW

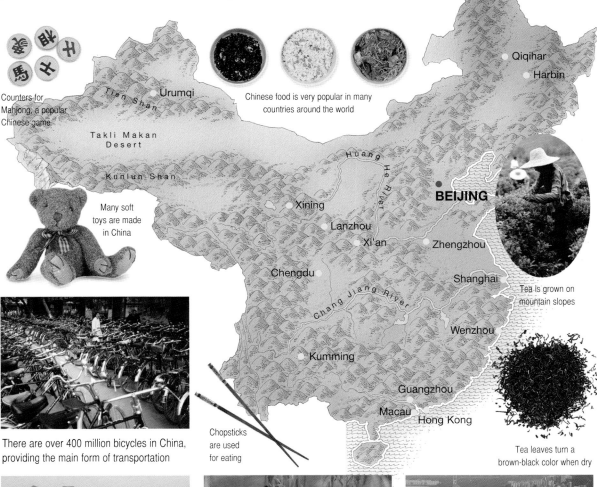

Counters for Mahjong, a popular Chinese game

Chinese food is very popular in many countries around the world

Many soft toys are made in China

Tea is grown on mountain slopes

Tea leaves turn a brown-black color when dry

There are over 400 million bicycles in China, providing the main form of transportation

Chopsticks are used for eating

The Great Wall of China is 4,500 miles long. Some parts were built 2,000 years ago

Giant pandas have to eat for 12 hours a day to get enough nourishment from bamboo

Hong Kong is an important business center with the world's busiest deep-water port

Tibet

Known as 'the Rooftop of the World', Tibet is set in a plateau high up amidst the Himalayas.

Population:	2.5 million
Money:	Renminbi
Language:	Tibetan
Hello:	Tashi delek
Pronunciation:	tah-shi de-leh

Mongolia

The 'Land of Blue Sky' has very little rain or snow but winters are long and very cold. Most Mongolians are nomadic herdsmen, living in round, white-felt tents, keeping herds of goats, sheep, horses and cattle. They are very proficient horsemen – the children learn to ride before they learn to walk!

Horses are an extremely important part of everyday life in Mongolia

Population:	2.7 million
Money:	Tugrik
Language:	Mongolian
Hello:	Sain Bainuu
Pronunciation:	sain bai-nau

North Korea

The rugged mountains of North Korea are covered in dense forests, making agriculture difficult, so Koreans have reclaimed land along the coast to grow grain and rice. Mining is important in North Korea. One of the most important minerals mined here is tungsten, which has the highest melting point of all metals and is used to make lightbulb filaments.

Kimchi is a pickled vegetable dish flavored by chili, red pepper and garlic

North Korean schoolchildren playing a type of harp called a kayagum

Population:	23.9 million
Money:	North Korean won
Language:	Korean
Hello:	Annyong ha shimnikka
Pronunciation:	an-YOH HASHim-ni-kah

Taiwan

Taiwan has mountain peaks, coastlines of black volcanic rock and misty waterfalls. It also has lively cities, teeming with cars, motorcycles and people. Many electrical products such as hairdryers, TVs and DVDs are made here and exported around the world.

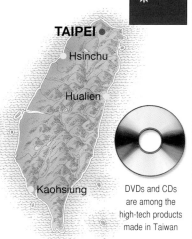

DVDs and CDs are among the high-tech products made in Taiwan

The National Palace Museum in Taipei holds a large collection of Chinese artefacts

Population:	23 million
Money:	Taiwan dollar
Language:	Chinese
Hello:	Ni hao
Pronunciation:	nee haOW

South Korea

The seas around South Korea teem with life, so fishing is an important industry. Koreans process seaweed, extracting chemicals that are used in foods, cosmetics and clothes. South Korea is the largest producer of computer chips in the world. The biggest holiday is on September 12, when Koreans visit the graves of their ancestors.

Seafood

Seaweed is widely eaten

Ships of all sizes are built here, including oil tankers, fishing trawlers and passenger liners

Population:	48.4 million
Money:	South Korean won
Language:	Korean
Hello:	Annyong ha shimnikka
Pronunciation:	an-YOH HASHim-ni-kah

Japan

Japan is known as 'the Land of the Rising Sun' and it is one of the richest countries in the world. There are many successful high-tech businesses making cars, televisions and computer games – Japan is the world leader in the production of computer games and the leading manufacturers are all based here. Tokyo is a major financial center. Active volcanoes and tsunamis – huge waves up to 22 feet high – can cause damage to the country, which also has about 1,000 earthquakes a year (so earthquake resistant buildings are very important). Shinto is the traditional religion of Japan, and people worship the sacred spirits in the form of the sun, mountains, trees and rocks.

Motorcycles and cars are made in Japan

Flower-viewing picnics are held in April and May, when the cherry trees are in blossom

The Kinkaku-Ji Temple in Kyoto is a beautiful Buddhist temple

Mount Fuji is a sacred mountain in the Shinto religion

Martial arts have always been popular

Hokkaido

Sapporo

Akita

Sendai

Niigata

Honshu

Mt. Fuji ▲

TOKYO

Kyoto

Nagoya

Shizuoka

Yokohama

Kobe

Hiroshima

Osaka

Fukuoka

Shikoku

Kochi

Kyushu

The traditional sport of sumo wrestling

Famous for...

Fishing
The Japanese catch (and eat) more fish than any other country in the world

Sushi
Beautifully presented raw fish is a popular dish

Sumo wrestling
Wrestlers try to make their opponents touch the floor. These athletes eat a huge amount of food to add bulk to their bodies

Kimono
These are robes with wide sleeves fastened with a sash

Computers and games
Japan is the world leader in the development of computer games

Technology
Many new products, such as digital cameras, were invented or improved here

Population:	**127.9 million**
Money:	**Yen**
Language:	**Japanese**
Hello:	**Konichiwa**
Pronunciation:	**koh-NEE-cheewah**

'Bullet trains' travel up to 186 miles per hour. They are very clean and efficient

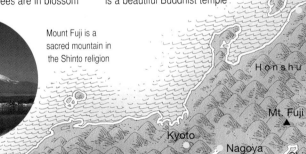
Much of Tokyo was rebuilt after the 1923 earthquake and the Second World War

Australia

This is the world's largest island, measuring 2,500 miles across. 65% of the country is 'outback' – flat plains that are some of the hottest and driest places on earth. Most people live in towns and cities along the southern and eastern coasts, and the Great Dividing Range Mountains separate these fertile areas from the drier climate inland. Australia is one of the world leaders in mining, exporting huge amounts of coal, as well as gold and diamonds. High-tech farming means that the country is almost entirely self-sufficient, with huge cattle and sheep farms producing dairy products, meat and wool. A quarter of the world's wool is produced here. Outdoor sports are popular in Australia, particularly sailing, surfing, rugby and cricket.

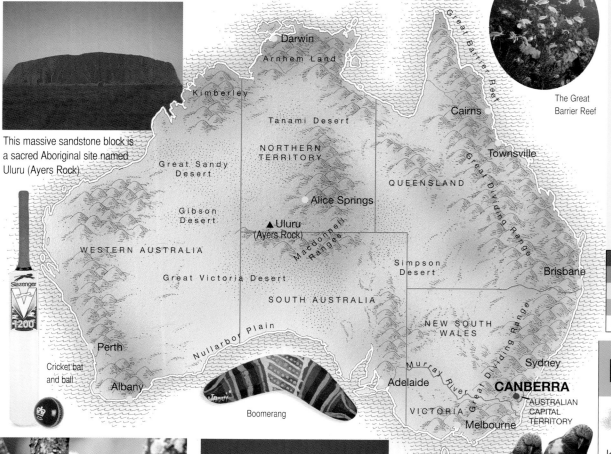

The Great Barrier Reef

This massive sandstone block is a sacred Aboriginal site named Uluru (Ayers Rock)

Darwin
Arnhem Land
Kimberley
Tanami Desert
NORTHERN TERRITORY
Great Sandy Desert
Gibson Desert
Alice Springs
▲ Uluru (Ayers Rock)
Macdonnell Ranges
WESTERN AUSTRALIA
Great Victoria Desert
SOUTH AUSTRALIA
Nullarbor Plain
Perth
Albany

Cairns
Townsville
QUEENSLAND
Great Dividing Range
Simpson Desert
Brisbane
NEW SOUTH WALES
Murray River
Sydney
Adelaide
CANBERRA
AUSTRALIAN CAPITAL TERRITORY
VICTORIA
Melbourne
TASMANIA
Hobart

Cricket bat and ball

Boomerang

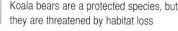

Koala bears are a protected species, but they are threatened by habitat loss

The uniquely-shaped Sydney Opera House is one of the busiest arts centers in the world

Colorful birds can be found in many parts of the country

Kiribati

● **BAIRIKI**

Kiribati is a group of 33 tiny tropical coral islands. The people fish, farm seaweed and grow coconuts.

Population:	**93,000**
Money:	**Australian dollar**
Language:	**English**
Hello:	**Hello**
Pronunciation:	**hel-lo**

New Zealand

The islands of New Zealand are known for their natural beauty. Rotorua is one of Earth's wonders, with hot springs, geysers, bubbling mud pools and colored lakes and pools. Most people live on North Island and work in the service industries, but agriculture is also very important. Pine forests produce timber for furniture and wood pulp for paper making. Cattle are raised for meat and dairy products.

Auckland
Rotorua
North Island
Palmerston
WELLINGTON
Blenheim
Christchurch
Southern Alps
South Island
Dunedin

Spectacular waterfall

The wool from sheep is used to make clothing and carpets

Kiwi fruits

Population:	4.2 million
Money:	New Zealand dollar
Language:	English
Hello:	Hello
Pronunciation:	hel-lo

Tonga

Only 40 of the 170 islands of Tonga are inhabitated, and most of these tropical islands are covered in lush rainforest. Farming is the most important industry, and the main export crops are pumpkins, coconuts, vanilla pods and bananas.

Vanilla pods and coconuts are grown here

NUKU'ALOFA

Population:	101,000
Money:	Pa'anga-Tongan dollar
Language:	English
Hello:	Hello
Pronunciation:	hel-lo

Samoa

The islands of Savai'i and Upolu are hilly with dense rainforest. Most people in rural areas are self-sufficient, growing crops and fishing for food. The main exports are hardwood timber and coconut cream.

Savai'i
APIA
Upolu

Rugby is a popular sport on the islands

Population:	189,000
Money:	Tala
Language:	English
Hello:	Hello
Pronunciation:	hel-lo

Tuvalu

There are no rivers on these nine islands, so the people have to collect and store rainwater.

FONGAFALE

Population:	10,000
Money:	Tuvaluan dollar
Language:	English
Hello:	Hello
Pronunciation:	hel-lo

Nauru

At just 8 square miles, this is the smallest republic in the world. There is no capital city.

Yaren

Population:	10,000
Money:	Australian dollar
Language:	Nauruan
Hello:	A kamawirei
Pronunciation:	a kam-a-wir-ay

Micronesia

Yap Islands
PALIKIR

The name Micronesia means 'small islands' and is appropriate for this group of 607 islands. Exports include fish, black pepper and craft items. Oysters are farmed to produce pearls. On Yap, stone money is still used.

Pearls

Population:	111,000
Money:	US dollar
Language:	English
Hello:	Hello
Pronunciation:	hel-lo

Solomon Islands

This country is spread across 998 islands. The six main islands are mountainous and covered in dense rainforests. Forestry is the main industry, and timber the main export. The valuable wood is used for boatbuilding and flooring. There are active volcanoes on the Solomon Islands, and frequent earth tremors.

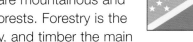

Shells are sold abroad and used to make buttons

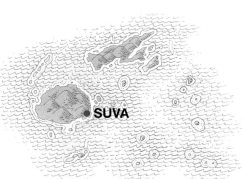

HONIARA

Population:	507,000
Money:	Solomon Islands dollar
Language:	English
Hello:	Hello
Pronunciation:	hel-lo

Palau

OREOR

Palau has six main island groups totaling over 300 islands. Tourists come to see the spectacular sea life, including giant clams.

Population:	20,000
Money:	US dollar
Language:	English
Hello:	Hello
Pronunciation:	hel-lo

Fiji

The 100 inhabited islands of Fiji are covered in forests or grassy plains. The people grow yams and rice to eat. Fiji also has 700 uninhabited islands, most of which are surrounded by coral reef. Tourists come here to see the huge shoals of colorful tropical fish.

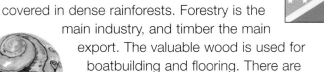

SUVA

Dolphins swim in the coral reefs

Population:	844,000
Money:	Fijian dollar
Language:	English
Hello:	Hello
Pronunciation:	hel-lo

Marshall Islands

This country consists of over 1,000 coral islands. All of the world's species of turtle are found in the seas here.

MAJURO

Population:	60,000
Money:	US dollar
Language:	English
Hello:	Hello
Pronunciation:	hel-lo

Papua New Guinea

Wewak

Madang

PORT MORESBY

Over 1,000 tribes live here, speaking 700 different languages. The largest butterfly in the world – the Queen Alexandra's Birdwing butterfly – is found in Papua New Guinea's rainforests. It often has a wingspan of more than 10 inches.

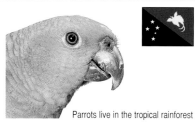

Parrots live in the tropical rainforest

Population:	6.5 million
Money:	Kina
Language:	English
Hello:	Hello
Pronunciation:	hel-lo

Vanuatu

These 80 islands are mountainous, with active volcanoes. The land is covered in tropical forests.

PORT-VILA

Population:	232,000
Money:	Vatu
Language:	English
Hello:	Hello
Pronunciation:	hel-lo

Antarctica

Antarctica was the last continent to be discovered. It is the highest, coldest and windiest continent on Earth, and is covered in a thick layer of ice that is 3 miles deep in parts. Antarctica has 90% of all the ice in the world. Air temperatures inland fall to −110° Fahrenheit and rise to −20° Fahrenheit in summer. Winds can be up to 190 mph. There is an international agreement to set aside Antarctica for research. Scientists come here to study the land, the sealife and the atmosphere.

Seabirds find plenty of fish in the seas

Lesser Antarctica ● South Pole

Greater Antarctica

Seven different species of penguin live and breed on the Antarctic coast

The Antarctic interior supports almost no life. Nothing grows but lichens and moss

Famous for...

Coldest recorded temperature
−129° Fahrenheit

Longest day
On December 21st, there is 24 hours of daylight

Sealife
The seas are full of tiny plants, providing plenty of food for fish

Whales
Seven species of whale live here

Arctic

The Arctic is a region rather than a country. It is formed from parts of Russia, Alaska, Canada, Scandinavia and Iceland. There is no solid land beneath most of the Arctic ice sheet. In summer, the ice sheet is mostly surrounded by sea. In winter, the ice extends to the mainland of the surrounding countries.

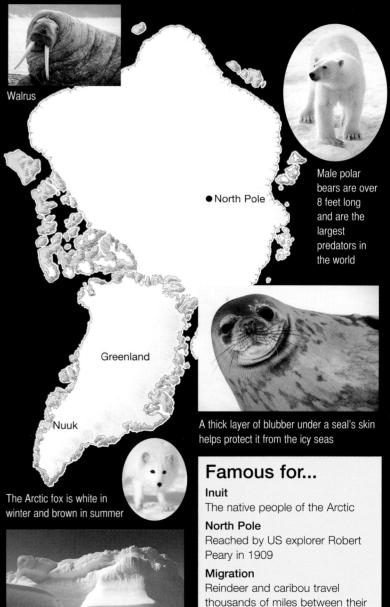

Walrus

● North Pole

Greenland

Nuuk

Male polar bears are over 8 feet long and are the largest predators in the world

A thick layer of blubber under a seal's skin helps protect it from the icy seas

The Arctic fox is white in winter and brown in summer

Icebergs break away from the pack ice in summer and can be a hazard to ships

Famous for...

Inuit
The native people of the Arctic

North Pole
Reached by US explorer Robert Peary in 1909

Migration
Reindeer and caribou travel thousands of miles between their summer and winter feeding grounds

Rich resources
Oil, copper and nickel have been found here

Overseas Territories

Several countries in the world govern places for strategic, economic or political reasons. These are called overseas territories.

Australia

Ashmore and Cartier Island

Christmas Island

Cocos Islands

Coral Sea Islands

Heard and McDonald Island

Norfolk Island

Denmark

Faeroe Islands

Greenland

France

Clipperton Island

French Guiana

French Polynesia

Guadeloupe

Martinique

Mayotte

New Caledonia

Reunion

St. Pierre and Miquelon

Wallia and Futuna

Netherlands

Aruba

Netherlands Antilles

New Zealand

Cook Islands

Niue

Tokelau

Norway

Bouvet Island

Jan Mayen

Peter I. Island

Svalbard

United Kingdom

Anguilla

Ascension Island

Bermuda

British Indian Ocean Territory

British Virgin Islands

Cayman Islands

Falkland Islands

Gibraltar

Guernsey

Isle of Man

Jersey

Montserrat

Pitcairn Islands

South Georgia and the Sandwich Islands

St. Helena

Tristan da Cunha

Turks and Caicos Islands

USA

American Samoa

Baker and Howland Islands

Guam

Jarvis Island

Johnston Atoll

Kingman Reef

Midway Islands

Navassa Island

Northern Mariana Islands

Palmyra Atoll

Puerto Rico

Virgin Islands

Wake Island

Index

Index

Index

Index

Acknowledgements

Photography: p.8 Quetzal, Ralph Lee Hopkins (Lonely Planet), p.9 Hummingbird, Margarette Mead (Getty Images), p.9 Cars, Trevor Wood (Getty Images), p.9 Havana, Tom Bean (Getty Images), p.10 Steel drums, Oliver Benn (Getty Images), p.12 Bogota, Krzysztof Dydynski (Lonely Planet), p.12 Palacio Salvo, Wayne Walton (Lonely Planet), p.12 Rainforest, Greg Caire (Lonely Planet), p.13 Polo, Phil Weymouth (Lonely Planet), p.28 Oil rig, Mark A. Leman (Getty Images), p.28 Skier, Terje Rakke (Getty Images), p.29 Helsinki, Stephen Saks (Lonely Planet), p.29 Lake, Graeme Cornwallis (Lonely Planet), p.29 Street, Anders Blomqvist (Lonely Planet), p29 © Inter IKEA Systems B.V. 2008, p.31 Bicycles, Mark Downey (Getty Images), p.31 Windmill, Hindeo Kurihara (Getty Images), p.31 EU, Neil Beer (Getty Images), p.32 TGV, Chris Kapolka (Getty Images), p.36

Black Forest, Josef Bek (Getty Images), p.36 Traditional house, Doug Armand (Getty Images), p.37 Austrian Alps, Neil Beer (Getty Images), p.37 Hallstatt (Getty Images), p.38 Prague, Anthony Cassidy (Getty Images), p.38 Warsaw (Getty Images), p.39 Romanian market, Rhonda Gutenberg (Lonely Planet), p.39 St. Andrew's Church, John Noble (Lonely Planet), p.41 Bazaar, Grant V. Faint (Getty Images) p.41 Carpets, Robert Freck (Getty Images), p.42 Catherine's Palace (Getty Images), p.43 Snow leopard, Tim Davis (Getty Images), p.44 Citadel, Thomas Schmitt (Getty Images), p.44 Dead Sea, Hugh Sitton (Getty Images), p.44 Iranian women, John Borthwick (Lonely Planet), p.44 Al-Aqsa, Siqui Sanchez (Getty Images), p.45 Mecca, Nabeel Turner (Getty Images), p.46 Petra, Jon Arnold (Getty Images), p.46 Sayyida Ruqayya Mosque, John Elk III (Lonely Planet), p.48 Mumbai, Eddie Gerald (Lonely Planet), p.49 K2, Ed Darack (Getty Images), p.49 Truck, James Strachan (Getty Images), p.51 Hindu Temples, Dennie Cody (Getty Images), p.51 Petronas Tower, Josef Beck (Getty Images), p.52 Brunei, Robin Smith (Getty Images), p.52 Fruit vendors, Paul Chesley (Getty Images), p.52 Planting rice (Getty Images), p.54 Mongolians, Paul Harris (Getty Images), p.54 Palace Museum, Mark Downey (Getty Images), p.54 Korean children, Tony Wheeler (Lonely Planet), p.55 Sumo wrestlers, Chris Cole (Getty Images).

Additional photography by Richard Brown.

Many thanks to Betty Wass, Jeanne Tabachnick, Herbert Lewis, Earl Gritton and Stephen Volz for the use of their photographs of Africa, and to Leonardo for the use of their photographs from tourist boards around the world.

Thanks to the following tourist boards for the use of their photographs: Dominican Republic, Nicaragua, Kenya, Netherlands, Spain, Portugal, Thailand, New Zealand and the Seychelles.

We would also like to thank Penny Boshoff for her research, CIRCA for their data and the CIA for the use of their flags from the World Factbook.